Woody Herman

JAZZ MASTERS SERIES

Woody Herman

STEVE VOCE

Selected Discography by
Tony Shoppee

For Louise, Susie, Ian and Catherine

First published in Great Britain in 1986 by
APOLLO PRESS LIMITED
11 Baptist Gardens, London NW5 4ET

© Steve Voce 1986

British Library Cataloguing in Publication Data
Voce, Steve
    Woody Herman.—(Jazz masters series; 11)
    1. Herman, Woody   2. Jazz musicians—
    United States—Biography
    I. Title   II. Shoppee, Tony   III. Series
    785.42'092'4   ML419.H/

ISBN 0-948820-03-9

Series editor: David Burnett James

Typesetting by Concept Communications, Crayford, Kent

Printed and Bound in Great Britain by
Anchor Brendon Limited, Tiptree, Essex

Contents

Acknowledgements

The sources of most of the material in the book are listed in the bibliography. However, it could not have been written without the kindness and invaluable help so unstintingly given by Alun Morgan and Tony Shoppee. Alun and Peter Clayton have been particularly generous in letting me make use of their published research, and Eddie Cook, publisher of *Jazz Journal International*, has made every aspect of that magazine's resources available to me. Additional help has come from my friends Alan Appleton, Jim McMaster, Ron Clough and Nancy Frey; and I have been allowed into Woody Herman's great family through the reminiscences of his and my friends, the musicians Nat Pierce, Joe Temperley, Shorty Rogers, Bill Berry, Phil Wilson, Bobby Lamb, Don Rendell, Marc Johnson and Eddie Harvey. Tony Shoppee, Alun Morgan and my wife Jenny painstakingly plodded through and corrected the manuscript's grammar — or lack of it.

S. V.

Illustrations

Dear Steve ———

I am looking forward to reading the book.

Regarding retirement, I am too old to retire — however I am still younger than the President. Ronald Reagan!

Thanks,
your friend

Woody Herman.

'Nobody does what Woody does as well as he does. If we could only figure out what it is he does . . .'

Phil Wilson

Woody Herman's main influence on jazz was felt through the effects of the First Herd, the Second Herd and the band of the middle sixties. It is on these bands that I have allowed the emphasis of this book to fall.

Steve Voce

Chapter One

'Nobody ever needed to be bored working for Woody Herman,' said one of his sidemen, 'because his soloists are so good that it's like going to a great jazz concert every night.' On the face of it, that could almost be a summary of Herman's career. The idea of 'a great jazz concert every night' reflects the fact that, despite the tribulations and inevitable traumas of keeping sixteen men on the road for 48 weeks each year, one never heard of a bad concert by one of Woody's bands. Despite his unique reputation as a generous and gentle employer of 'friends', Herman has always displayed the highest standards of professionalism, and these standards are always reflected in his bands on stage. Off stage Woody acknowledges that jazz musicians are exuberant and often highly strung, and he knows exactly how far to let them unwind through horseplay and humour. A supremely stable person himself, he has managed to keep control of some of the most eccentric musicians that jazz has known without ever appearing to exert authority. 'Woody's great talent,' said one of the band, 'is to keep out of the way.'

One of the keys to his success is his appreciation of and ability to talk to young people, both in his band and as fans of his band. 'Young people think constructively and move forward,' he says. 'Too often old people are bound up with nostalgia and simply want to live their early lives over and over again. You can't do that. Whilst we'll acknowledge the past and play *Woodchopper's Ball* when we're asked, we've got to have new things happening in the band all the time. Our young men are creative people, and my job is to nurture that quality, and to provide a platform for its development.'

'Young people think constructively and move forward.' Photo David Redfern

The Herman Herds have been the incubator for more talented
soloists than any other jazz organisation. There are many reasons for
this, including a high turnover of band members. Duke Ellington's
band, for example, enjoyed long periods of stability when the sections
stayed the same. Consequently Duke's band produced only a handful of new soloists, albeit some of them amongst the best in the world.
Woody, perhaps because his kind of operation meant that he couldn't
pay high wages or perhaps just because of the rigours of life on the
road, had a high level of movement in and out of the band with a
consequent higher level and variety of talent to be discovered in his
ranks. After half a century of almost uninterrupted travel round the
world one can see the wisdom of his admonition 'Be not disen-
couraged, brother!'

Woodrow Charles Herman was born in Milwaukee on 13 May

1913. His teacher at St. John's High School was Sister Fabian Riley, and each year he takes the band back to Milwaukee to play a benefit for Sister Riley's scholarship fund. But Woody was not destined to spend the normal years at school. By the time he was six he began singing and dancing in the local theatres, and by the age of eight he was touring professionally and appearing at theatres throughout the Middle West with his father. He must have been pretty good, because he had literally stopped shows with his singing and dancing.

'The very first song I sang in the theatre was a lulu called *You Should See My Gee Gee From The Fiji Isles*. I finally recorded it 30 years later at Capitol under the name of "Chuck Thomas And His Dixieland Band", because I didn't have the courage to come out in the open with it. We speeded the tape up so that it put me a tone or two higher. The record company did a campaign on it in certain areas of the country and it sold a fantastic amount in those places. But then they suddenly decided that the lyric was too risqué and it got banned on a couple of networks. It hadn't seemed like that when I was eight. It was just a little boy singing a hot tune. Little Woodrow was swinging.'

Woody's next move was into a kids' group working vaudeville theatres and movie halls. Their role was to provide a prologue to the movies, and they acted out Booth Tarkington stories, led by a boy called Wesley Berry who was in the Jackie Coogan mould. With the money Woody earned from these activities he bought his first alto saxophone and later a clarinet. The idea was that he should study these with a view to using them in his stage act, but Woody had grander horizons in mind. Eventually, encouraged by his parents, he graduated to being a single act and featured the two horns when he was billed as 'The Boy Wonder Of The Clarinet'. Like drummer Buddy Rich, Woody was virtually raised in the theatre, but as he grew older he became more interested in wider fields of music and began playing with groups of musicians when he was about 14. Right away he got the band bug and didn't want to return to vaudeville. His parents were most upset. They felt that while Woody was in the theatre he was an artist, but playing in a band was an entirely different matter.

During all this Woody somehow still found time to go to school, but his love of bands had taken root. The booking agencies in Chicago used to issue brochures about their individual bands, and Woody collected them avidly, and soon knew them all off by heart.

Even then he dreamed of the day when he would have his own band. It was to be a basically hot band with a big brass section (in those days that meant three or four men, and when the first Herman band was formed it in fact had five brass).

While still at high school he joined the Myron Stewart Band, a local group resident at Milwaukee's Blue Heaven Club. Later he moved to Joey Lichter's Band where he was featured as a vocalist and soloist. Lichter was a jazz violinist from Chicago, and it was here that Woody had his first real encounter with jazz.

Leaving Lichter, he persuaded his parents to let him leave home and join the society band of Tom Gerun, and here he played alongside baritone saxist Al Morris, who later made his name and fortune as vocalist Tony Martin. Another one destined for bigger things was the band's vocalist, Ginny Sims. Woody was featured on tenor. 'I sounded like Bud Freeman with his hands chopped off,' he remembers.

Gerun was a man of some courage. One night while he was leading the band on the stand in Pittsburgh a telegram was brought to him. It was from his business advisers in New York to tell him that his financial interests had just been wiped out in the Wall Street Crash. That night, to celebrate, he threw a big party for the band.

After four years with Gerun Woody joined Harry Sosnik's band, and later Gus Arnheim's where Bing Crosby had at one time been the vocalist. While with Arnheim he was approached when the two bands were playing at the same theatre to join Isham Jones's band. Since he had friends in the band, trumpeter Pee Wee Irwin and trombonist Jack Jenney, he agreed and some months later he moved to Isham.

Isham Jones was a remarkable man, talented as a song writer, band leader and multi-instumentalist. He also wrote his own arrangements for his bands at a time when it was more usual to use 'stocks', stereotyped arrangements sold by the music publishers. Whilst Woody was later to have a hit with *Woodchopper's Ball*, Isham had recorded *Wabash Blues* in 1922 and sold almost two million copies. He composed *I'll See You In My Dreams*, *It Had To Be You*, *On The Alamo* and many other top quality hit songs.

While he was prepared to put up with a man appearing for a job in the wrong band uniform, he showed no such tolerance when it came to the music and if someone missed a cue or played a wrong note, he had been known to invite them out the back to settle the matter. Apparently bloodthirsty, he used to love it when his musicians fought and would always watch without intervening.

Victor Young played violin and arranged for the band, as did Gordon Jenkins, who described it as 'the greatest sweet ensemble of that time or any other time'.

There seem to have been two definite directions within the band, the sweet and the hot. It was here that Woody made his first jazz recordings, leading a small group for Decca under the titles of the Swanee Swingers and Isham Jones's Juniors. The band made six very respectable sides between 25 and 31 March 1936. *I've Had The Blues So Long* was one of five Herman vocal features and sounds very much like the records of the later Herman Band That Plays The Blues. On *Slappin' The Bass* Woody's clarinet has an agile, stinging quality reminiscent of Goodman, and Chelsea Quealey's muted trumpet echoes Muggsy Spanier. Frankie Jaxon's *Fan It* was to be a hit with the Woodchoppers ten years later. Here it was distinguished by Woody's vocal and some good solos. Elsewhere Virginia Verrell's vocals dampened the heat of the session, but generally it was a good debut for Woody.

The two definite directions were given their head when Isham suddenly decided to retire in the middle of 1936. One of the violinists formed part of the band into a 'sweet' band and Woody led a nucleus determined to head into the 'hot.'

It was to be five years before the Woody Herman Band as it was to be known would become profitable. The years in between were to be tough and very lean with work hard to come by, and in 1941 Herman said that if he'd known how hard it was going to be he would never have gone ahead. Later on it became impossible to form a big band without having a backer to put up a large sum of money to run it until it began to earn. Woody and his men had no backer, so they formed a co-operative, a practice frowned upon by the American Federation Of Musicians, with equal shares for the nucleus of ex-Isham Jones players. These were Woody, trombonist Neil Reid, violinist Nick Hupfer, trumpeters Clarence Willard and Kermit Simmons, tuba player Joe Bishop, bassist Walter Yoder, tenor saxist Maynard 'Saxie' Mansfield and drummer Frankie Carlson. Each man put up a similar amount of money and later other musicians, like pianist Tommy Linehan, were invited to become members. Neil Reid was

Charlotte and Woody in the late 1930s. Photo Dave Dexter Jr.

the treasurer, and it was his job to keep expenses to a minimum and pay out wages to the hired musicians who were not members of the co-operative. This was never easy in a band that worked an average of two nights a week and four nights in a good week. Walter Yoder managed the band — a role later designated 'straw boss'.

One of the most important events in Woody's life happened that year. He'd known the red-haired Charlotte Neste since they were both 17. She was working under the professional name of Carol Dee when they met in San Francisco, and they married in New York on 27 September 1936, 'right after Prohibition'.

'We got married at the toughest time when things were breaking the worst,' Charlotte told *Down Beat* magazine. 'But maybe that's the best time to get married — at least we think so.'

Charlotte was right for, despite the fact that Woody spent so much time on the road, theirs was one of the happiest of marriages right up to her death in 1982. Loved by all the musicians in the bands and friends with many of them after they left, she must have been the most popular band leader's wife of all time.

Throughout the autumn of 1936 the new co-operative worked at putting the band together. Three of the arrangers from Isham's band, Joe Bishop, Gordon Jenkins and violinist Nick Hupfer, started writing a library of charts, and the co-operative began auditioning necessary sidemen. It seems likely that these were amongst the last auditions Herman ever held, for in later years he took musicians on by recommendations from colleagues, usually former members of his band.

Joe Bishop abandoned his tuba and took up fluegel horn, probably becoming the first jazz musician to use the instrument, which was more limited than the trumpet, but had a nicer tone. Bishop had an expressive but circumscribed range and it was decided, whether by Joe or the co-operative is not clear, that the fluegel was for him.

Things went well at first. After six weeks' rehearsal the band was ready and immediately two golden apples fell into its lap. It was given a recording contract by Decca Records and two nights after its first recording session on 6 November it began a two week engagement at the Roseland Ballroom in Brooklyn. As if that wasn't an auspicious enough beginning for such an embryo band, there were local radio broadcasts from the Roseland.

The first recording session used two tunes, *Wintertime Dreams* and *Someone To Care For Me*, which were dogs. The prim, straight tempos went well with Woody's routine vocals, and there wasn't the slightest hint that the band would ever be anything but anonymous and insipid.

On 10 November they cut *The Goose Hangs High,* hardly a jazz classic, but there was a good jazz vocal from Woody and some mellow playing from Bishop both in solo and in the section.

After the job at the Brooklyn Roseland was over the band moved to the New York Roseland, where they shared the billing with another equally unknown band led by a pianist called Count Basie.

The band stayed in New York for the next four months, working at the Roseland and cutting a handful of records for Decca. The shape of things to come was mapped out when they recorded *Dupree Blues* and *Trouble In Mind* on 26 April 1937. The Herman style loosely

15

paralleled the Dixieland two beat of Bob Crosby's band, but Herman's singing on these two blues showed an affinity with that kind of music normally only found in the work of black performers. In this respect he's always shared the honours with trombonist Jack Teagarden, perhaps the only other white musician to really get to the roots of the blues.

Trouble In Mind is a classic blues written by the lengendary Richard M.Jones and a hit during the twenties in the recording by Bertha 'Chippie' Hill and Louis Armstrong. Since then the song had fallen from popularity and it proved ideal material for Woody. It opened with a stinging clarinet solo in the Artie Shaw manner and then Woody sang the vocal with a gruff obbligato from Joe Bishop's fluegel. Compared with Chippie Hill's original graveyard-orientated tempo, the Herman version almost bounced. *Dupree Blues,* better known in early days as *Betty And Dupree,* was enhanced by another mellow obbligato from Bishop, a fine plunger muted solo from Reid and solos from Saxie Mansfield and Bishop. It is interesting to note how, as always, the saxophone solos have dated whilst the brass ones remain fresh. Woody told the sombre tale with a forceful vocal and the performance, paired with the band's version of Jelly Roll Morton's *Doctor Jazz,* sold well over the ensuing years. The formula for The Band That Plays The Blues had been worked out, if not yet fully applied.

Perhaps the best chance to evaluate the early Herman band is offered by the radio transcriptions they recorded when they returned from their first tour, which took in the Eastern states during June 1937. The recordings were made on 23 September, and by this time an extremely important change had been made. Tommy Linehan replaced Horace Diaz at the piano chair. Linehan was from Massachussetts, and had played with well known bands there and along the East coast from 1928 onwards. He was a quiet little man with a neat moustache, his appearance not reflecting a commitment to jazz and boogie woogie piano that was unusually effective for the time. Later his piano sound was to become one of the trade marks of the band, notably in pieces like *Blues Upstairs, Blues Downstairs, Chips' Boogie Woogie, Indian Boogie Woogie* and the blues library.

Radio transcriptions are an invaluable reference for the jazz historian, for they often provide musical documentation of the various bands at times when they were forbidden to make recordings, by

16

union bans or, as in the case of the 1937 transcriptions, at a time when the band didn't otherwise record prolifically. The mixture of titles recorded on 23 September gives us a good idea of the elements in the repertoire. There were the jazz standards, *Muskrat Ramble, Jazz Me Blues, Ain't Misbehavin', Squeeze Me* and *Weary Blues;* the quality standards, *Exactly Like You, Can't We Be Friends?, Someday Sweetheart,* and a couple of lesser known songs of the day, *Remember Me* and Hoagy Carmichael's *Old Man Moon.* The emphasis is always on the jazz aspect of performance, although it is sometimes a little questionable as in the introductory clarinet passage to *Exactly Like You,* where it has to be owned that Woody has a touch of Ted Lewis about him. However, this is swept aside by a heavily attacking trombone solo from Reid, a fastidious trumpet solo from Clarence Willard and some finally righteous wailing from Herman.

Remember Me has some ponderous tenor from Mansfield before a solo of great delicacy from Bishop. The influence of New Orleans clarinettist Jimmy Noone with his limpid and full tone remains evident in Woody's playing today (oddly enough Noone's phrasing is often prominent in Herman's alto playing as well as in his clarinet work) and it can be heard in *Can't We Be Friends?,* otherwise a fairly routine performance.

The Dixieland numbers smack of Bob Crosby's performances, with Woody, Neil Reid, Bishop and Mansfield the main soloists. It's interesting to note that at this time Herman was technically the best of the soloists.

Towards the end of 1938 Woody re-evaluated the band's musical policy. Whilst they were good at playing Dixieland numbers, Bob Crosby did it better. The band wasn't in the same league as Jimmy Lunceford or Duke Ellington, both of whom were to be big influences later on. What did they do well? They played the blues. On 22 December a small group from the band titled Woody Herman And His Woodchoppers recorded *River Bed Blues.* Hyman White had just joined on acoustic guitar, and this was his debut. He complimented Linehan to perfection, and his solo playing had the bluesy intimacy of Teddy Bunn's work. The Band That Plays The Blues was under way.

A couple of weeks later Horace Stedman 'Steady' Nelson arrived on trumpet, filling out the section to three. Although he had made his musical debut with Peck Kelly's band in Texas in 1933, he was a devotee of the Ellington band, and he brought a ferocious growl style which was to provide a contrast to the more gentle playing of Joe Bishop.

Confirming the commitment to emphasis on the blues, George Simon recalls that, when the band played at Frank Dailey's famous Meadowbrook Ballroom, it filled its radio shows almost entirely with blues. These weren't so popular when the band played at the Rice Hotel in Texas, either. The manager sent a note up to Woody on the stand which read 'You will kindly stop playing and singing those nigger blues.'

On 12 April 1939 Woody took the band to Decca in New York for the recording session which was going to change all of their lives. Woody had discovered early the painful economics of trying to run a big band. No matter how good things were, resources always seemed stretched. But then came that recording session. There was a new girl vocalist to sing *Big Wig In The Wig Wam*, Mary Ann McCall, one of the most musical singers ever to grace the band and a lady who was to return to make it on a big scale with the Herd in the late forties.

The band recorded a fast, bouncing blues that Joe Bishop had written. It was called *At The Woodchopper's Ball*. After the opening riff, Woody played a stylised clarinet solo which has become a part of the number, and everyone who plays the piece uses that solo. Reid had a brooding trombone solo, Mansfield booted the tenor and Steady growled. Walt Yoder and Hy White walked together for a chorus and then the now familiar build up of riffs came, at this time without the soaring clarinet that Woody was later to impose on the final chorus. 'It was great,' says Woody, 'the first thousand times we played it.'

In the middle of the summer the record took off, and that first version sold a million copies. Woody has played *Woodchopper's* every night since, and the various Herds recorded it many times.

If it hadn't been notable for *Woodchopper's*, the 12 April session would have still been noted for a fine plethora of blues performances. *Dallas Blues* had another sombre and beautifully poised trombone solo from Reid and a biting solo from Woody that began with a paraphrasing of Johnny Dodds' solo from King Oliver's *Dippermouth Blues*. *Blues Upstairs* and *Blues Downstairs* are outstanding amongst all the blues charts that Joe Bishop contributed. After Linehan's cascading piano introduction, Hy White plays a filigree single note guitar solo and then Linehan introduces a mournful chorus of fluegel

18

before Woody's classic twelve bar verses. Linehan has a fine boogie woogie-based solo to lead into the by now familiar build up of riffs. Turn the 78 over and *Blues Downstairs* turns out to be a continuation. Woody has his Noone-Bigard hat on for his solo, and is followed by Neil Reid, sounding more like Floyd O'Brien than ever. The rockpile of riffs begins early and closes on Woody's clarinet break. Most of the jazz fans of the forties will remember this coupling note for note! A month later two more notable tracks with rather more sophisticated arrangements, *Casbah Blues* and the non-blues *Farewell Blues* were recorded. As far as Woody was concerned, 'Blues' was the in word.

At last, the band began to make money. The blues permeated 1940 with the key word figuring in the title of the ballad *Blue Prelude*, composed by Joe Bishop and Gordon Jenkins, and first recorded by Woody with Isham Jones. As you would expect from Jenkins, composer of such superb ballads as *Good Bye*, this was a beauty, and Woody's vocal one of his most elegant yet. The band was fattened out with a second trombonist and the great Cappy Lewis came in at the end of 1939. Trumpeter Lewis had an incisive and delightful style which was to be a tremendous asset to the band for the next three years. His is something of a Herman dynasty, for his son Mark Lewis has been in the Herman trumpet section since the beginning of the eighties.

Chapter Two

From the evidence of his earliest recordings with Isham Jones, Woody Herman's clarinet playing had always been both eloquent and self-assured. In the early days it was possible to tell which other players had caught his ear. Jimmy Noone, the languid and fat-toned prime mover from New Orleans, was a main influence, and Jimmy's expert use of trills remains an element in Woody's work to this day. Regardless of Woody's devotion to all things Ellingtonian, Duke's clarinet player Barney Bigard would have inevitably been a major source of inspiration for him. Barney's sound was more facile and jazz-committed than Noone's, but he had the same singing New Orleans quality (Barney's nick name was 'Steps', and Woody deliberately emulates him in the Woodchoppers' record of that name made in 1946). Apart from Bigard's specific sound, Woody made use of his methods, and his famous declamatory soaring over the final choruses on many of the Herd's performances echoes the way in which Duke used Barney's sound to fly across the Ellington band ensemble.

In the pre-forties period one can hear Woody occasionally switch onto someone else's style. He was accomplished enough to do a Goodman or a Shaw or even, as we have noted, a Ted Lewis! But by 1940 the elements had come together and, although the Noone and Bigard influences were to remain discernable, Woody had blended them into his own distinctive sound. Perhaps the best example of it from this period is the 1941 *Woodsheddin' With Woody*, a fast moving Lowell Martin chart to feature Herbie Haymer on tenor and Cappy

Lewis on trumpet as well as Woody. Here also the Basie influence is revealed as Linehan, White, Yoder and Carlson open with the familiar tight and sparse rhythm section sound. Although he was never to eliminate them in the way that the genius Barney Bigard did, Woody had achieved an ability to negotiate the breaks between the registers so that not even another clarinettist would notice them. This is a sure sign of a gifted musician, and the solo on *Woodsheddin'* might have been regarded as a virtuoso display were the listener not side-tracked by the fact that it is a searing hot display of swinging jazz clarinet. It also held another formalised aspect of Woody's style which was to be used to great effect in the ensuing years — the exciting growl from the throat used with random abandon by Pee Wee Russell and honed to exciting perfection by Edmond Hall.

One always thinks of Woody as a clarinet player first, and yet he feels more at home playing the alto saxophone, and indeed his playing of this is far more sophisticated than his clarinet work. At the same session that produced *Woodsheddin' With Woody* the band re-corded *Bishop's Blues*, a tribute to Joe who by this time had contracted tuberculosis. It opened with a glorious alto solo which at that stage reflected almost as much of Charlie Holmes's playing as it did that of Johnny Hodges. But Hodges was probably Herman's all time favourite, and his later work on alto always acknowledged the Rabbit.

Despite the fact that he was so much in thrall to the Duke, Herman has always been an eclectic listener both to soloists and to bands. (His eagerness to hear the newly-formed Earl Hines band at Chicago's Grand Terrace produced mixed results. Woody was knocked out by the exciting new sounds and then knocked up by a gangster who shot him in the leg shortly after he left!)

Herman's playing, notably on clarinet, has needed little modification with the passing of the years, and it is quite remarkable to hear him soloing, for example, in the same context as Andy Laverne's electric keyboard. But then Woody has never been afraid to follow what his ears tell him, and it's typical of him that after hearing John Coltrane playing soprano one night, he went out the next day and bought a soprano for himself and this third horn has been a feature of his work during the eighties. 'In the old days when Sidney Bechet and Johnny Hodges were about the only people who played soprano, it was a terrible horn to conquer,' he said. 'But now you can buy a good horn that stays in pitch and it's much easier to cope with it.'

Woody's qualities as a blues singer have already been noted, but his vocal talents were wide enough to ensure that, had he not been a band leader or horn player, he could have made it as a leading vocalist. As well as the blues and the novelty numbers like *Get Your Boots Laced Papa, Who Dat Up Dere?* and the famed *Caldonia*, he had a subtle poise and timing that enabled him to sing ballads to tremendous effect, and the 1941 *'Tis Autumn* reveals a singer entirely devoid of the cloying histrionics which instantly dated many contemporary ballad performances. Interestingly his voice has dropped over the years, although perhaps not quite by the octave that he claims. Throughout the years he has recorded many jazz-inspired ballad performances, perhaps most notably Ralph Burns's arrangement of *Laura* for the First Herd in early 1945. The skilful Burns had written a glorious mattress for the band to place first under Woody's alto and voice, and then under Bill Harris's trombone for a legato display which showed that when he wanted to Harris could tread with ease the ground usually regarded as Tommy Dorsey's preserve.

But we digress. By 1941 the arrangers were beginning to shape the band sound to a far greater degree. Previously much reliance had been placed on 'heads', but when Deane Kincaide and Jiggs Noble joined Joe Bishop on the arranging team, the emphasis changed. First of all came Noble's re-working of *La Cinquantaine*, which was a feature for drums and clarinet and a massive hit under the title *Golden Wedding*. Unfortunately Bishop's health deteriorated and he went into Saranac Lake Sanatorium at the beginning of October 1940. But before going he handed in the score of a new blues, *Blue Flame*, a brilliant moody 12 bar which the band cut for Decca in February 1941 and which has remained Woody's theme tune to this day.

Jiggs Noble was now Woody's staff arranger and scored the band's more commercial material. There was by this time quite a lot of this, and the erosion of the Band That Played The Blues had begun. The standards of the sidemen were raised appreciably when musicians like trumpeters Ray Linn and Billie Rogers and tenorist Herbie Haymer joined the ranks. Herbie Haymer had quit Jimmy Dorsey's band because he wasn't being given enough solos to play, a situation that Woody was happy to put right.

The band moved west to California in the summer of 1941, and an initial short booking at the famed Hollywood Palladium was extended to three months. Then it moved to the Sherman Hotel in

Chicago for a couple more months before fetching up at the Strand Theatre in New York.

The New York theatre bookings were notorious amongst the musicians in the big bands. A band would play up to six shows a day between film showings, starting work at nine in the morning and finishing after midnight.

'It was like doing time up the river,' Woody remembers. 'Some of those engagements would last for about ten weeks and would include the week-ends. It was a very difficult and tough existence, and we'd lose one or two guys every week. They became ill or they just became natural basket cases from over indulgence and so forth. Of course there was a lot of panic all the time, because in those days the rule was that the show must go on, and it did.'

It's very easy to see how musicians could take to drink to find some release from such tension, and understandable that they hardly felt inspired to play. Bud Freeman recalls that 'Playing *One O'Clock Jump* at nine thirty each morning was as relaxing as working in a steel foundry.' Bud played for Goodman and Tommy Dorsey, and they must have been much more difficult to work for than the easy going Herman. Dorsey, for example, had a system of fines for his musicians which included a $50 one for being late on the stage. (One night when one of his violin section missed the first three numbers by being late, Tommy called him out in front of the audience and made him play his third violin part for each number as a solo!) And the Dorsey band played up to *nine* shows a day. Sometimes Tommy would call a band rehearsal as well!

There was a lot of showbiz hokum involved with playing to the fans, or bobby-soxers as they then were. Among the other New York theatres Herman played at were the Capitol, Loew's State and the Paramount. The Paramount had a superior lighting system and of course the familiar rising stage, so that the band would start playing somewhere in the bowels of the theatre and emerge slowly before the audience like some primeval monster from the deep. Woody's band played *Blue Flame* of course, and as it came up on the riser, as it was known, Herman had his back to the audience. As the point of the clarinet solo entry was reached Woody turned round in the total darkness and began to play with phosphorescent paint covering his hands and his clarinet! He stood it for a week, but after that the paint had gone.

September 1941 saw the recording of *Blues In The Night*, a major hit which was issued on a 78 with *This Time The Dream's On Me* as backing. This latter was another good example of Woody's way with ballad lyrics.

Joe Bishop came out of hospital in January 1942 and worked from home as an arranger for the band. His playing days were over, but he wrote for Woody and others until ill health in 1951 forced his retirement from music. That same month the band cancelled a string of 17 one-nighters and returned to Hollywood to make its first movie, provisionally titled 'Wake Up And Dream' but finally issued as 'What's Cookin?'. The band played *Woodchopper's Ball* and the Andrews Sisters were among the many variety acts featured. With the film in the can, the band began working its way back from Hollywood to the East when Frankie Carlson was struck with appendicitis. Dave Tough came into the band as a substitute, and it is entirely likely that he was the drummer on the four titles that the band recorded on 28 January. These included *A String Of Pearls* and three ballads, which make it difficult to find any distinctive touch from the drummer, whoever he may be.

In March 1942 Saxie Mansfield finally left the band and music altogether. This was another move away from the Band That Plays The Blues, as Mickey Folus moved in from the Artie Shaw band to replace him. The band spent the spring playing at the Hotel New Yorker before moving to the Paramount Theatre for the summer.

By this time the draft into the American armed forces was playing havoc with the band personnel and it seemed to Woody that there were farewell parties every day.

'Every time you turned round someone else had gone as the guys were drafted out from underneath us. You never knew who was in the band, and at one time it was so bad we were almost halted. There was also this wartime hysteria of trying to do five or six shows a day as well.'

Although it still worked under the tag of the Band That Plays The Blues, the library by 1943 included a number of much more complex charts that made greater demands on the musicians. Still unswerving in his devotion to Duke Ellington, Woody hired Dave Matthews to write for the band. Dave already had a prodigious reputation amongst musicians as a man who could write convincingly in the Ellington style, and he was very experienced, having come through the ranks of the Ben Pollack, Jimmy Dorsey, Benny Goodman and Harry James bands during the previous decade.

But as had always been the case, Woody was ready to open the door to new and untried talent. 'One guy who wrote a couple of charts for us around that time came into the band as a temporary trumpet for a week. When it was over I recommended him to stick to arranging. That was one of my wilder judgements. It was Dizzy Gillespie!'

Gillespie's writing already had the shape of things to come as can be heard on the 1942 Herman recording of *Down Under*, which Dizzy wanted for some obscure reason to dedicate to Australia. He also wrote *Swing Shift* and *Woody 'n' You* but neither went into the library, although it seems likely that *Swing Shift* appears as a theme on one of the band's contemporary broadcasts.

During the seventies Woody asked Dizzy to up-date these arrangements for the current band, but Dizzy had no interest in going back. Their careers have crossed on occasion. Once when Woody was snowbound in Salt Lake City with his band, Dizzy flew in for a job, but the rest of his band were trapped elsewhere by the weather. So the Herman band appeared as the Dizzy Gillespie Band with Woody in the sax section!

The band was also much influenced by the work of the Jimmy Lunceford and Count Basie bands at this period, and the standards of the men coming into the ranks needed to be higher to cope with the more advanced writing. Surprisingly, since so many musicians were being swept away in the draft, the standards *did* go up.

In the middle of 1942 James C. Petrillo, President of the American Federation of Musicians, imposed one of his two long bans on musicians recording for the commercial companies. Had it not been for the survival of some of the permitted recordings for radio (and these did not emerge before the public until decades later) a vital period of jazz history would have been lost to us, a period when the Ellington band was burgeoning, when the spores of bebop were taking hold, and when the Herman band was filling up with new talent. More sophisticated charts laid a bigger burden on the brass, and Woody took on girl trumpeter Billie Rogers, thus becoming one of the first leaders to use five trumpets. Billie was featured as a soloist and vocalist as well as working in the section where the extra strength allowed trumpeters to rest in turn.

Woody has recalled how, with the continuing stream of farewell parties in the band at that time, Billie could start the evening as fifth trumpet and by the time it was over have worked her way up to the first trumpet chair as the men got loaded and fell off the stand. Billie was the first girl to sit in the ranks of an American name band, and she was not there merely as a novelty. Her main inspiration was the trumpet playing of Roy Eldridge, and she really wanted to play jazz. Unfortunately the Petrillo ban meant that she was in the band when it was playing better than ever before, but not recording. It was not until the eighties when a collection of her broadcasts with Herman appeared in an album that we were able to judge just how good she was. Later she married the band's manager Jack Archer, and finally left Woody in January 1944 to form her own band. There were some questions about her contract with Woody, and a five month wrangle ensued before the AFM found in her favour.

Other future stars of the jazz firmament began to pass through the sections. Tommy Linehan's health was not good, and his eventual replacement at the piano was Jimmy Rowles, a man who was to return to later Herds and who became a quite outstanding soloist and accompanist. Vido Musso broke up his own band and he and Pete Mondello came in on tenors. One of the most powerful of jazz trumpeters, Nick Travis, made an early but brief appearance. Skippy DeSair joined on baritone and was to stay through the triumphs of the First Herd. Still with the band were veterans Neil Reid, Walt Yoder, Hy White and Frankie Carlson.

The band returned to Hollywood in January 1943 to make a full length film, *Wintertime,* with glamorous ice skater Sonja Henie. Her spectacular beauty was the main feature, but there was plenty of space for music and the band played four feature numbers including *Dancing In The Dawn,* later extracted from the film and issued on a V-Disc. This was a long number ranging in mood from the sentimental to the hard swinging by way of an added string section and vocal chorus, vocals from Woody and Carolyn Grey, a tough tenor solo from Vido Musso and a burning clarinet improvisation from the Chopper. The band appeared in heavy furs, overcoats and scarves, and Woody wore ski boots and a lumberjack outfit. Hardly suited to balmy California!

Walt Yoder and trumpeter Chuck Peterson were soon drafted, and Gene Sargent came in on bass. He also wrote arrangements and one of them, *Basie's Basement*, was later recorded for Decca. Frankie Carlson was one of many to be seduced by the California climate, and he handed in his notice. The band's new singer, a young girl called Anita O'Day, had similar ideas, as did Vido Musso and altoist Les Robinson, and they left. Neil Reid's reason for going was more pressing as he was inducted into the Marines.

The replacements came from somewhere. Woody wasn't a predatory band leader, but he suddenly found himself with two of Charlie Barnet's best men, Barnet's erstwhile and excellent drummer Cliff Leeman and, most significantly, Greig Stewart 'Chubby' Jackson on bass. Trombonist Ed Keifer joined from the Bob Chester band, from whence another trombonist, Bill Harris, had recently gone to join Benny Goodman.

Amongst all this coming and going in the middle of 1943, the fine altoist Johnny Bothwell and, more importantly, one of Woody's best ever girl singers, the late Frances Wayne, came into the band (some years later Frances married Neal Hefti, trumpeter and arranger with the First Herd).

The band criss-crossed the country with one nighters. Wartime conditions made travel difficult, with the trains crammed with servicemen and bus services reduced. Woody, who has always been a keen motor racing enthusiast, travelled by car and enjoyed it, but still the stress of the times got to him and he collapsed from nervous exhaustion in Philadelphia in October 1943 and didn't return for a couple of weeks.

As the AFM was still haggling with the record companies, the band couldn't record for Decca, but it did record some splendid radio transcriptions in November that year. Later Decca *was* able to issue these and the titles cut before the emergence of the fully fledged First Herd in late 1944 have been unjustly obscured by the incandescent success of the later band. Presumably with Duke's agreement, Woody used some of the Ellington cornerstones on these sessions, notably tenorist Ben Webster and altoist Johnny Hodges. *Basie's Basement*, among the first titles to be recorded, featured Webster, and Ben joined the band again in New York for a session in January 1944. This produced eight titles including the hit *Noah*, with Woody's rasping vocal and pungent plunger-muted trumpet from Cappy Lewis. Ben was featured on five of the tracks and blew one of his breathy masterpieces into *Crying Sands*, a beautiful ballad by the new

Herman with Ralph Burns. Photo Jazz Journal International

bass player, Chubby Jackson. This also featured a rare alto solo from Johnny Bothwell, who, like Woody, was obviously a Johnny Hodges fan (Hodges himself recorded *Perdido* with them in April that year).

The band had a new pianist, a man who was ultimately to change it out of all recognition. He had been with a small group led by vibraphonist Red Norvo and earlier with Charlie Barnet. He was to become one of the great figures in jazz. His name was Ralph Burns.

Ralph was to be associated with Woody for many years, but many other great jazzmen passed briefly through the early 1944 band. Allen Eager, Herbie Fields, Budd Johnson and George Auld all sat in the tenor chairs. Ernie Caceres participated in one of Tommy Dorsey's many on-stage rows and left forthwith to join Woody on alto, and Ray Nance and Juan Tizol joined the Ellingtonians who recorded for Woody. Tenorist Vido Musso came back briefly when the band made the film *Sensations Of 1945*, where the band shared the music with Cab Calloway and his orchestra. As filming finished Cappy Lewis got the dreaded request from Uncle Sam and left after almost five years with Woody. Guitarist Hy White, the last of the original members of the Band That Plays The Blues, left to become a teacher.

An era ended.

Chapter Three

Despite the never ending questions about the possibility of their return, the big bands never really went away. Admittedly they were crushed by heavy taxes and the advent of television in the second part of the forties, but the format proved resilient and there are probably more big bands today than there were during the golden era of big bands in the forties.

The First Herd, as the next Herman band was to be known, was probably the highest point in Woody's career. Although George Simon had referred to the band of the early forties as 'the herd', the name really stuck and became an identifying mark with the band of 1944—6.

There are few absolute standards in jazz. The music has developed so rapidly over the last 70 years that a yardstick is out of date as soon as it is created. No wonder when one considers the fact that jazz musicians have examined and extrapolated every facet and device developed in 'classical' music over the last 500 years. The inevitable telescoping that has taken place has led to many blind alleys and, to be honest, the odd musical charlatan or two. So, whilst one person might claim, for instance, that Miles Davis is the greatest jazz trumpeter who ever lived, his view has no more substantial weight than another person who might say that Miles Davis was not a jazz trumpet player at all. In jazz the opinion of the individual listener is as important as that of the musicians or those who write about jazz. In classical music, where weight and profundity have found their levels over the centuries, standards are vastly more established and accepted, and one would be unlikely to find the eminence of Brahms or Beethoven, for example, taken in question.

With that in mind, it is not possible to assert that the band led by Duke Ellington in the period around 1940 is the greatest big band there ever was. Suffice it, then, to say that it seems likely that it was. Ellington, unlike Herman, had been able to select his musicians with care over the years, and each one had grown into his role in the orchestra. The Ellington combination had almost everything. Firstly, there was Duke's writing. At any point in his career, even if he was relaying trashy pop songs or rescoring the horrible *Mary Poppins* for the band, there was always something of interest, something to be learned from the writing. Ellington ranked with the greatest composers and orchestrators of his century. Then there were the men in the band, soloists of giant stature who were the first jazz musicians to have music specifically written for them as individuals. Ellington knew how each of them would respond to any musical situation he chose to create for them, and in Cootie Williams, Rex Stewart, Barney Bigard, Johnny Hodges, Joe Nanton, Ben Webster and Harry Carney, he had what might have been the greatest permanent collection of jazz improvisers ever assembled. The bright flare of Jimmy Blanton's bass playing which lit the jazz sky for such a brief episode provided both a stimulus to Duke's writing and a pivot to spin the band on, as he forged new lines with his revolutionary approach.

No wonder that Woody was drawn so powerfully to Ellington's music, and it was this edition of Duke's band that permeated the whole band scene in the first half of the forties.

As we have seen, the Herman men had also been influenced by the rhythm geniuses of the Count Basie band, and they must have noted if not been able to emulate the fluent and relaxed playing of the giants like Lester Young and Buck Clayton, Harry Edison and Buddy Tate.

Technical skill of a very high degree was now required of any sideman, and nowhere was it more in evidence than in the brilliant ranks of the Jimmy Lunceford orchestra. Whereas Ellington handcrafted his section sound so that any one of the individuals could be singled out from it, the Lunceford band was so precise and well drilled that each section sounded like one instrument, and indeed the band sound dominated, with great soloists like Willie Smith, Joe Thomas and Trummy Young subordinated to it. Once that

Lunceford standard had been set, every band was judged against it, and the Lunceford proficiency was something else for the Herman band to aim at.

Bebop was somewhat tenuously established by the time that the First Herd came together, and Woody's new band was amongst the first to reflect the new music's influence. Drummer Dave Tough was with some other men from the band when they had their first exposure to the music on 52nd Street in 1944. The band they heard was one of the very first to define the new music, and it was led by Dizzy Gillespie and Oscar Pettiford. Tough told Marshall Stearns 'As we walked in, see, these cats snatched up their horns and blew crazy stuff. One would stop all of a sudden and another would start for no reason at all. We never could tell when a solo was supposed to begin or end. Then they all quit at once and walked off the stand. It scared us.'

Tired of what they saw as the limitations of conventional improvising, young men like Gillespie, Pettiford, Charlie Christian, Charlie Parker, Bud Powell and Thelonious Monk eschewed variation on written melody in favour of a rigorous and wide ranging investigation of the chords on which those melodies were based, chords which up until now had been merely signposts provided by the pianist when he accompanied. This kind of playing resulted in the casual jazz listener being locked out, and the resultant complaint that the listener 'couldn't hear the tune'. This would also be the kind of playing that 'scared' Tough and his colleagues. But not for long, because within a year they would be blending the bebop styles and methods into the music of the Herd.

This was the musical stage then that was ready for the emergence of the First Herd.

The First Herd seemed to arrive suddenly in the middle of 1944. In fact key members like Ralph Burns and Billy Bauer had joined by the beginning of that year and Chubby Jackson and Frances Wayne had joined Woody in 1943, but it was appropriate that the band made its remarkable impact only when the fully assembled group began work.

Chubby Jackson, ebullient, irrepressible and highly charged with nervous energy, became the focal point of enthusiasm in the band when he joined from Charlie Barnet in September. Chubby had been with Barnet when the band had included Ralph Burns, Neal Hefti and Frances Wayne, all to join the Herd in subsequent months, presumably largely on Chubby's recommendation. Burns, only 21, brought his extraordinary talents to the band in December, and immediately began writing the library which was to ensure the Herd's place in the jazz history books. In January 1944 Neal Hefti took over the trumpet chair that Cappy Lewis had left (Cappy returned after his military service) and guitarist Billy Bauer joined to replace Hy White in March.

In April Cliff Leeman handed in his notice. He was a fine player, adept at all the drummer's roles and a man who listened to the soloists and gave them sensitive support. Replacing him presented a problem. Woody wanted to take on Dave Tough, a veteran who had been a member of the Austin High School gang in Chicago during the twenties where he had been a colleague and friend of Bud Freeman, Eddie Condon and Frank Teschemacher. After a long bout of illness which was to recur throughout the rest of his short life he had joined Tommy Dorsey's band in 1936 and then moved to join first Bunny Berigan and later Benny Goodman in 1938. He was the main agent in persuading Bud Freeman to leave Tommy Dorsey and join him in Goodman's band, an event that caused a huge commotion in the music business at the time and led to a very public slanging match between Goodman and Dorsey. Freeman regretted the move ever after. Bud's association with Dave was a close one and they had many interests in common outside music. They made a trip to Europe together in 1928, and it was only natural that when Bud formed his Summa Cum Laude Orchestra, Dave should be on drums (natural too that the sensitive Freeman should exclude Eddie Condon for a time on the grounds that he drank too much, but hardly compatible with Tough's penchant for the same foible!) But the significance of Tough's association with Freeman is to be found in the recording session made by a pick up band called Bud Freeman's Famous Chicagoans on 23 July 1940 in New York. Jack Teagarden, the trombonist, had left his big band in Philadelphia after the gig the previous night and had travelled all night to be there. When the session began trumpeter Max Kaminsky hadn't shown up and the first two tracks were made without him. While these handicaps may not have been unusual, they hardly portended the magnificent recording session which was to follow. The ensemble sound created by Kaminsky's direct trumpet lead, Pee Wee Russell's wild and yet concentrated clarinet sound and the remarkable manner in which

Teagarden and Freeman were able to fill out the band without getting in each other's way, was quite without precedent, and the rhythm section couldn't have been bettered, with fine work from the under-rated Dave Bowman and monumental drumming from Tough.

Repeated listening shows how vital Dave was in binding the band sound together, rocketing the horns into their solos, and all the time keeping a sizzling rhythm performance going, drums prominent throughout without ever once intruding. This was a performance of great significance, and it is odd that it went unremarked at the time. Certainly it could not have reached the ears of Chubby Jackson when Woody suggested Davey as a replacement for Cliff Leeman. Woody appreciated Chubby's enthusiasm and did all he could to foster it, even to the extent of hiring musicians solely on Jackson's recommendation. But Woody wanted Tough. He had used him as a substitute for Frankie Carlson on one occasion in The Band That Plays The Blues, and knew how versatile and suited to the Herman music he was. Chubby was horrified. He regarded Tough as a player from a bygone era and was determined that his hiring would be a retrograde step in a band that Jackson wanted to be progressive. It could be that, since Tough was in the navy until the time he joined Woody on his discharge, Chubby had never heard the drummer play. Subtle as ever, Herman let the matter drop and didn't sign Tough on immediately. But at the next rehearsal to help some new men bed in and to try out some new charts, Tough turned up with his drums. He played and, according to legend, at the end of the session a tearful Jackson threw his arms around Tough's puny frame and embraced him with delight. One of the greatest rhythm sections of all time had come together.

Because of the tremendous potency of his arranging and composing, the fact that Ralph Burns was a tremendous jazz pianist has sometimes been neglected. Yet he was able to swing harder than most, and when supercharged by the Jackson-Tough-Bauer cartel he was uncatchable. He was a great stage setter for the faster numbers and his opening solos from the earliest ones onward continuously reveal how great was his responsibility for the ordering of the Herman sound. Whilst many of the young musicians of the day had simply grafted a veneer of bebop onto the older swing styles, Burns had a good grasp of the new music by 1944, and he wove it into both his solos and into his scores for the band. Able by now to command a brass section with almost Lunceford-like qualitites, he was particularly able to create exciting, incandescent music for it, and must take some credit for the imposing parade of iron men who were to play lead trumpet in succeeding years. Such was Ralph's value to Woody as the custodian and creator of the band's library that after the first year Woody took him off the piano chair and hired a replacement, keeping Ralph solely to write for and when necessary rehearse the band.

Ralph's contributions to Woody's library were to continue years after he had left the organisation. His gifts were such that they were wasted travelling the roads with a band, and, after a few sophisticated and creative jazz albums under his own name, later years found him immersed in the world of film and television music and of more commercial recordings.

Sam Marowitz took the lead alto chair in April 1944 and was to stay until the First Herd broke up. Later John La Porta, at one time emerging as a good bebop clarinet soloist before that instrument went out of fashion, came in on second alto. But before that, in April, Joseph Edward 'Flip' Phillips joined. Flip had substituted for Vido Musso in the earlier band. He was already something of a veteran, having begun his career as a clarinettist in the middle thirties. He had worked with trumpeter Frankie Newton at Kelly's Stables in New York for a year before switching to tenor sax in 1942. When Vido left, Flip was the obvious replacement, but Woody had difficulty in persuading the tenor man to join. 'I had a hard time getting him,' Woody told George Simon, 'You know why? He didn't want to leave Russ Morgan's band. *That* represented security!'

When he did join, Flip's lean, aggressive tenor soon became one of the band's trademarks. He was a shouter in a shouting band, and pitched against some of the finest brass jazz had so far seen, he needed the declamatory style and hard swing that he had developed. Like Ben Webster he could be lush and seductive on the ballads, and he swiftly built up a following that was to stay with him during his succeeding years with the Jazz At The Philharmonic unit. Still a splendid solo player, his work is enjoying new popularity in the eighties. In August 1984 a Woody Herman reunion was held in Boston for all the ex-Herdsmen who lived in that area or who could get there. Woody and Chubby were there along with Dave McKenna,

Jimmy Giuffre, Bill Berry, Chuck Wayne, Al Cohn, Nat Pierce, Phil Wilson and Flip. 'Flip looked truly great,' said Wilson. 'At 69 he looks like a healthy 55 year old and is truly playing better than ever before in his life. And he has a wonderful calm, satisfied demeanour.'

At 28, Flip was comparatively old among the ranks, but the average age came down again when 21 year old trumpeter Pete Candoli arrived. Later dubbed 'Superman With A Horn', Candoli was a man with a huge range on his instrument and great staying power. He sat alongside young Neal Hefti in the section, and like Hefti he was capable of turning out a creditable arrangement. Candoli had an incredible track record for his age, having worked in the bands of Sonny Dunham, Will Bradley, Benny Goodman, Ray McKinley, Tommy Dorsey, Freddy Slack and Charlie Barnet before coming to Woody. Neal had also come from the Barnet band where he had been one of the chief arrangers as well as a featured soloist. He had joined Woody briefly in February 1944 for the filming of *Sensations Of 1945* and stayed in California for six months before joining the band on a permanent basis in August. Neil began writing for the Herd at once and shared with Burns the job of building the band's character. It was immediately obvious that his writing talents were exceptional and later on he followed Burns into the studio scene, writing for television and films. But unlike Burns he kept up his involvement with jazz and his prodigious involvement as a writer for the Count Basie Band of the fifties and sixties has been detailed by Alun Morgan in his book on Basie in this series.

A month after Pete Candoli joined, in midsummer 1944, the final and most important horn man joined the Herd. Willard Palmer Harris, trombonist superb, outlandish character and a man who was to be a major influence on jazz trombone playing until the present day. 'Woody always loved trombone players,' recalls Phil Wilson, 'and I was always grateful for that. But the relationship that built up over the years between him and Bill Harris was something special. It was a deep friendship that transcended the music business.'

Harris was a remarkable man in every respect. He led the band from the trombone section, and with all the brass in full cry he could be heard distinctively in the section. 'He could blow metal fatigue into the horn,' said Bobby Lamb, a man who was to sit next to Harris in the section of a later Herd. Bill was a kind and generous friend often providing support and shelter for lesser players in the trombone

Flip Phillips. Photo Max Jones

section. He was also a man full of remarkable contradictions. On the one hand he was very shy. When he was in England in 1959 with Woody's Anglo-American Herd, all the leading trombonists in London contributed to buy a gold cigarette lighter for him as a tribute. They had it especially engraved and arranged a ceremony for the presentation. They all turned up. Bill didn't. He was too shy.

But sometimes he wasn't shy, and his sense of humour is legendary. Trumpeter Bill Berry, himself an avid Harris fan and collector of Bill's records, remembers being in the trumpet section when the band played at an air force base in California. Afterwards the band was invited to the officers' mess for drinks. When Berry got there he found Bill Harris at the bar, drink in hand, in conversation with one of the officers. Bill had his band jacket and tie on, but no trousers. He must have had a thing about trousers. In later years Bill was one of two white musicians in an otherwise black edition of Jazz At The Philharmonic. This was in the early fifties and the group was on tour in Germany. They arrived at a hotel where rooms had been booked in advance for them. But the manager told them that there had been a mistake and that the rooms had been let to other visitors. As the musicians turned and walked away the manager ran after Harris and the other white musician and with a certain lack of subtlety told them that *their* rooms had been kept. Harris's colleague turned away with an oath, but Bill turned and went back with the manager. He walked into the lounge which was crowded with reclining guests. He moved to the centre of the room and placed his suitcase on the floor. He took off his coat, folded it, and put it on the suitcase. He unfastened his trousers and let them fall to his ankles. Then he made one of his famous strange noises, pulled up his trousers, put on his coat, picked up his suitcase and walked out of the hotel after the rest of the band.

On another occasion Woody was fronting the band and when he turned round he noticed that there were four trombones where there should have been three. Harris and Red Norvo had collected a couple of tailors' dummies from somewhere and Bill had dressed one in a band uniform and given it a trombone. He had tied the dummy's arm to his own and he was leaning forward explaining the music to it and telling it to stand up when he did. Later Bill and Red threw the other dummy from the roof of a penthouse with the result that police cars and ambulances came rushing to the scene.

Bill Harris was one of the most exciting jazz soloists of all time. His playing was both original and totally unpredictable. All of his solos on the records the First Herd made for Columbia are outstanding, even within their exciting context. The fact that many more versions of the same numbers survive in recordings for radio is a great boon for the jazz listener, since he always seemed to have improvised his solos afresh each time a piece was played. Often, when playing a piece night after night a musician will develop a set solo, useful if he is tired or out of inspiration (Johnny Hodges's *All Of Me* is a prominent example) but Harris seemed always able to create something new. Several bandleaders insisted that once a solo was established and particularly if listeners were familiar with it from records, it should not be changed by improvisation. Ted Heath and Tommy Dorsey are examples of such leaders, and indeed Buddy de Franco was fired by Dorsey for changing the solo on *Opus One* when he'd been told not to. 'But Tommy, it's not creative,' protested Buddy. 'You go and be creative on someone else's band,' snarled Tommy. A very different attitude to Woody, who was always eager to encourage the soloists.

Harris was in the Herman band from 1944 to 1946 and then again from 1948 to 1950 and from 1956 to 1958 with several shorter stays in between before settling in Las Vegas, where he found lucrative work with a small band led by Charlie Teagarden. Towards the end of his life he moved to Florida, living near to his old friend Flip Phillips, and the two men had a band playing locally until Bill's death in Miami from a heart condition on 20 August 1973. He was only 56.

Few musicians are able to develop a viable solo style that is wholly original, and Bill's way of shouting against the rest of the band echoed the glorious freedom and exuberance of Jay C. Higginbotham and Dicky Wells, but there the similarity ended. Bill made great use of contrasting dynamics, smeared and staccato notes, now prowling now ripping through the band with a bucketing solo.

'We were playing in Child's Restaurant one Sunday in 1956 when I'd been with Woody for about four months,' trombonist Bobby Lamb remembered. 'At that time we were using bass trumpet, and although Cy Touff is an excellent player, I was never fond of the instrument. Bill suddenly appeared to rejoin the band, and Woody asked him to sit in. Woody called for Johnny Mandel's *Not Really The Blues*, which is a real powerhouse of a number. So Wayne Andre and I set up to go through our usual routine. Suddenly there was this explosion! Bill played so strongly that Wayne and I just sat there gaping with amazement and let him get on with it. He led the whole band from the trombone section. It didn't matter how loud Woody's five trumpets played, if Bill thought something should go that way, it went that way!

'We roomed together for a year on the road, and it was like a father and son relationship. I was in a daze most of the time, couldn't believe my ears. He was also an excellent reader and a kind and communicative teacher, despite the fact that he was a shy and retiring man. Not nervous, mind you, but a man who said what he meant and didn't waste time with niceties. He had a tremendous sense of humour, and I think he should be remembered with a twinkle in the eye.'

The 1945 recording of *Bijou* was a latin feature for Harris. Woody refers to it as a 'stone age bossa nova'. It was a superb showcase crafted by Ralph Burns and if all the earlier recordings hadn't already done so, it displayed the Harris style and confirmed him as the major trombone influence of the forties along with the more staccato and less emotional playing of Jay Jay Johnson. Phil Wilson encountered the number in a later Herd.

'Woody used to have the succeeding trombonists play *Bijou* and both Bob Brookmeyer and I have recorded it with the band. I didn't like the idea because number one that's a hard act to follow, and number two, I'm Phil Wilson, not Bill Harris.'

Phil, who followed Bill into the band 20 years later, didn't know Bill well, but he did confirm Bill's reading ability and scotched the story of Bill being fired from the Benny Goodman band for lack of it. 'I'm sure that Bill would have been a good reader in Bob Chester's band, long before he joined Goodman. I can see that he and Goodman wouldn't get along, and it would have been a matter of personalities when he left.

'Incidentally, my history is by ear, which is the best way, and I remember hearing the story that Bill didn't take up the trombone until he was 22. That's not correct. The situation was that he actually played many instruments including tenor, piano and drums, but he didn't decide to specialise on one until then. Of course, he played both slide and valve trombones. Some of those old ballads he used to play, *Mean To Me* was one, were just mind boggling, they were so beautiful.'

Beauty coupled to humour. The concert stage had a ramp down

40

the middle. As the band finished *Northwest Passage* and the sounds died away, a plastic duck came waddling down the ramp quacking. Property of Willard Palmer Harris.

The next most important soloist to come into the band was also the most progressive in style. Trumpeter Saul 'Sonny' Berman was only 21 when he joined Woody, but by then he was a most experienced sideman. After joining Louis Prima in 1940 he played with the bands of Sonny Dunham, Tommy Dorsey, Georgie Auld (with Auld he recorded his first solo, a chorus on *Taps Miller*), Harry James and Benny Goodman. Berman's family had suffered a tragedy when his brother, who was also a musician, was killed in an accident when he was 17. Sonny himself died of a heart attack on 16 January 1947. He joined Woody in February 1945 and in the ensuing months made an enormous contribution to the band, particularly by way of his intensely creative solos which often changed the whole emphasis of some of the more commercial numbers like *Don't Worry 'Bout That Mule, A Kiss Goodnight* and *Uncle Remus Said*. His style was seated in the Roy Eldridge vein, and so it is not surprising that it took on Gillespian overtones in his last year. The recordings he made with the small group from the First Herd, the Woodchoppers, contained classic jazz from everyone involved, but if anything Berman was outstanding alongside Harris. Some of his muted work was excellent, ranging from the delicate to the pungent, and in September 1946 he recorded under his own name with a group drawn from the Herd for the Dial label. The music again proved to be a classic contribution for the time, and his lyrical contribution to Ralph Burns' *Nocturne* at this session demonstrated his great maturity. That maturity coupled to such fast and accurate technique showed a jazz giant in the making, and as in the case of trumpeters Fats Navarro, Clifford Brown and Booker Little who all died very young, we can only speculate on what might have been.

Woody told George Simon that Sonny was 'one of the happiest characters . . . What fire and feeling and warmth he had! And he was still just a kid. I remember once when we got to California he had saved around seven or eight hundred dollars, which meant he practically did without diamonds. One night he came to me to ask for advice. Should he put the money aside in case he wanted to get married in the future or should he buy "the longest, yellowest roadster"? We told him to get the car, so he went out and bought a

Cord. They weren't making them any more — in fact it was an older vintage than he was. Well, the first night he came to work the car was steaming and belching, and right away Sonny went over to Abe Turchen who was our road manager then, and asked him "What time is intermission, so I can go out and have an accident?" A few days later on the way to San Diego the car blew up completely.'

Unusually the band packed a vibraphone in its ranks, first played by Margie Hyams, and later Red Norvo, who arrived in December, 1945. Red had been a bandleader himself for many years (his last band had included Ralph Burns and his brother-in-law, young Shorty Rogers, later to join Herman) but had been discouraged by the way the style of his small group was wrecked by frequent departures of musicians to join the services. He joined Goodman for some months before leaving for Woody. With Woody he played a most important role in the sessions recorded by the Woodchoppers.

Until the release of its Columbia discs, the Herd's main exposure to its eager public came through broadcasts, and happily many of these have been preserved, so that we can hear the various elements coming together in the second part of 1944 that was to lead to the enormous impact that the band had in 1945 when it was able to blaze ahead with commercial recordings to add to the personal appearances and broadcasts. In July 1944 during a lengthy residence at the Hotel Sherman in New York, Woody signed an agreement to broadcast each Wednesday evening for the Columbia Broadcasting System in a show sponsored by Old Gold Cigarettes, and the Herman band took over from Frankie Carle's orchestra for a series that ran from 26 July to 4 October, eleven broadcasts in all and a very important exposure for the new library.

At this time George Simon was sent to New York to begin making V Discs for the services. These were non-commercial recordings produced specifically for the armed forces and were recorded without fee by the artists involved on the assurance that they would never appear commercially. Distributed generously throughout the various theatres of war many copies survived and of course all the jazz items involved have been subsequently made available on illicit labels. In an attempt to make the 12-inch records less attractive to the thief, violently contrasting forms of music were coupled together, so that for example V Disc 382 has Woody Herman's *Red Top* on one side and *Poor Little Rhode Island* and *Come With Me My Honey* by Guy

Lombardo on the other! Similarly, two earthy performances by blues singer Big Bill Broonzy are paired with *Clarinet Polka* and *Laugh Polka* by a band whose name will be allowed to lie peacefully in the murk at the bottom of the pond.

Simon approached Woody with a view to a session while the band was working at the Paramount theatre by day and the Meadowbrook Ballroom by night with the Old Gold Show thrown in. Simon was delighted to find Woody eager to record as much as possible for the troops and on 10 August, the first official sample of the First Herd's music was put on wax. Unfortunately the maudlin *There Are No Wings On A Foxhole* was one of the worst recordings Woody ever made, but soon to follow up were classics like *Apple Honey,* named after an ingredient in Old Gold's tobacco, and one of the famous 'head arrangements' that were to grace the Herd. These were put together by various members of the band working together and were not formally scored. In particular the individual sections would work out passages for themselves. *Apple Honey* was built on the chord sequence of *I Got Rhythm* and the recording for Columbia in February 1945 when coupled with another head *Northwest Passage* on a 78 record, became the band's first hit and music that was to embed itself permanently in the psyche of a generation of jazz fans.

The V Discs were mostly recorded in New York's Liederkranz Hall. Four decades on it is not surprising that any copies that still exist are pretty worn, and it is increasingly to the surviving broadcasts of the time that one turns for higher quality recordings. Many of the Old Gold Shows and the later Wild Root Shows (Wild Root was a hair cream, and the programme series was sponsored by the manufacturer) survive on tape. In addition to the previously mentioned cornucopia of alternative solos, the broadcasts provide an unmatched opportunity to study the sort of programme the band offered. On 2 August 1944 the Old Gold Show opened with *Flying Home*, another head arrangement featuring Ralph Burns, Flip and Woody, and some riffs which were later to find their way into *Apple Honey*. *It Must Be Jelly*, a Ralph Burns novelty creation for the voices of Woody and Frances Wayne came next, to be followed by another apparent lightweight, *Is You Is Or Is You Ain't My Baby*. But this last had powerhouse solos from Flip, Pete Candoli, Bill and Woody in a superb Burns chart that also used a passage that Ralph would later cannibalize for *Blowing Up A Storm*.

It has been mentioned that even when the setting was most trivial there was always something of interest in the writing of Duke Ellington, and the same is largely true of Ralph Burns. The Herman band played many of the ephemeral songs of the day, but frequently Burns' scores gave them an immortality which they did not in their pristine form deserve. And very often one of the solo giants would also ennoble the dross with the result that *Put That Ring On My Finger, I Wonder,* and *Katusha* assumed an importance out of proportion to their original weight. There is a fascinating example of this to be found in the various versions of the lightweight vocal feature for Woody, *Good, Good, Good* (the most outstanding is the remarkable direct line transcription on Fanfare 43-143) where, following the vocal, Burns has scored an orchestral ensemble in Bill Harris's trombone style, and the band rocks and lurches before confirmation comes in a bucketing and exultant break out by Harris himself. From a chirpy but insignificant opening the piece suddenly takes on the sublime exhilaration that only this band could impart to the listener. Another sophisticated device used by the band is obvious in the next track on the Fanfare album, *Goosey Gander,* an amalgam of the old tune *Shortnin' Bread* and the blues, where Flip Phillips's tenor sax solo is used to set the stage for a big shout up from Harris. Flip played a gentle, intricate solo to set the contrast ahead of the famous klaxon horn fanfare from the trombone section before Harris takes the stage for some mighty disembowelling! (All the surviving versions of *Goosey Gander* are notable for good Harris solos and a tremendous pile up of brass riffs in the final choruses. Also on display was the high note trumpet of Pete Candoli, the famous glissandi for the trumpet section and one of Dave Tough's eccentric drum tags, overrunning the coda by the band. On the less formal broadcast versions, Harris's solo is obscurely prefaced by Woody with the remark 'Ham sandwich and a bottle of beer'!)

Petrillo's squabble with the record companies came to an end in November 1944 and Herman switched from Decca to Columbia at the end of the year. The band's most famous titles were recorded in the Liederkranz Hall (where the V Discs had been made) in February and March 1945. Although these were the recordings that caused such a sensational enthusiasm and following for the band, they no longer represent the most accurate source for historians. Four of the broadcasts between February and July 1945 were recorded by a method described as 'class A direct line transcription'. Whatever this involved, the results were a clarity and presence that virtually amounted to high fidelity. Fortunately the recordings were mislaid or put away unplayed at the time, and they didn't surface again until the late seventies, when of course the LP medium existed and they were transferred with their original incredible and immaculate sound condition to two albums on the US Fanfare label (Fanfare 22-122 and 43-143). These albums are the most important evidence that we have of the band's greatness. Never have Tough's drums been so crisply presented, never has the brass been able to shout without distortion, never have Jackson's bass lines been so clearly heard through the ensemble, and never has Frances Wayne sounded better than in the two versions of her beautiful feature *Happiness Is Just A Thing Called Joe*.

Nonetheless the band's Columbia recordings caught the mood of the times with the war drawing to a close and the hope of a bright new future. People were ready for the exuberant turmoil, the powerhouse brass and the acceptable face of bebop as presented by the Herd. Returning servicemen who had heard the band on V Discs or on its relayed broadcasts wanted more, and the records sold on a massive scale. The individuals in the band began to sweep the board of the meaningless awards presented by the various music magazines, and as far as the public was concerned they became stars. Ralph Burns never quite overcame the embarrassment he felt when asked for his autograph. He couldn't see that his qualities made him more deserving of the 'star' appellation than many of the empty heads in Hollywood. Ralph was in his element, knowing that nowhere else would his work get the same treatment. He could bring a new chart to the band and immediately the music would take fire. He couldn't write fast enough. He concentrated on writing, and Tony Aless took over the piano chair.

Another writer came into the band, Shorty Rogers. For some weeks the fifth trumpet in the band had been Conte Candoli, but the school holidays ended and his mother made the sixteen year old return to school. He finally left school and returned in January 1945, but was drafted in September. Shorty Rogers left the army at the same time, and Conte was sent to the camp that Shorty had just come from. Red Norvo had recommended him to Woody, and Shorty walked right into the job.

'Everyone was influenced by Bird and Dizzy and was trying to bring their way of playing into the band. Neal Hefti and Ralph Burns and the other arrangers were marvellous to me, and it was like going to school, a graduate course, a real luxury. Pete Candoli took me in and watched over me like another brother.'

By now *Bijou* had been recorded as Harris's feature, and the band was knocking out other successes like Neal Hefti's *The Good Earth*, a beautifully constructed piece, typical of Hefti's high quality of output. *Caldonia*, a blues novelty that had come from Louis Jordan made its mark, and like *Woodchopper's Ball* and *Blue Flame* is one of the flag wavers that persists to this day. *Caldonia* was a collaboration between Burns, who wrote the opening and closing passages and Hefti, who wrote the lockjaw-inducing passage for the trumpet section. At the time Hefti's writing seemed insurmountable for the trumpets, but this was by now the most powerful trumpet section in the world, and it vaulted through Neal's tortuous creation. Incredibly, subsequent Herds play this passage faster and faster!

At the beginning of September 1945 Tough was briefly ill, and Buddy Rich took his place in a recording that produced the classic *Your Father's Moustache*. Rich's brilliantly accurate playing was different, but it produced the same results as he underpinned Berman, Harris and Herman to perfection. Harris barked a particularly gruff and splendid solo before Woody led the ensemble into a lyric that rivalled 'Ham sandwich and a bottle of beer' in its profundity. Chubby Jackson, who sported a five string bass, was usually the cheer leader in this kind of group activity, and his comedy work had earned him the radio billing 'Woody Herman and his band with Chubby Jackson and the Woodchoppers' as a fairly standard introduction. The Woodchoppers superseded the earlier Four Chips and was simply the generic name for any small band within the organisation.

In late 1945 the event which Woody described as 'the greatest thing in this man's musical life' occurred. Woody told Peter Clayton 'A mutual friend introduced our band via records to Igor Stravinsky in California. This man said he was going to get Stravinsky intrigued enough to do something about writing something for our band. I of course pooh-poohed it and thought it was ridiculous. I didn't believe Stravinsky would get involved with our kind of thing. Fortunately for me and the band I got a wire from Stravinsky saying that he was writing a piece for us and he hoped to have it finished by the Christmas season and it would be his Christmas gift to us.'

What Woody didn't tell Peter was that in fact, although he was kept unaware of it at this time by his accountant, Stravinsky was very short of money. The accountant called Woody and explained this and asked Woody if he would treat Stravinsky's piece as a commission. Woody did and paid for it. Stravinsky never learned of this.

Stravinsky completed the work, entitled *Ebony Concerto,* in Hollywood on 1 December 1945. He had added a harp and French horn to the band, and had employed a saxophonist to show him the fingerings on the unfamiliar instrument while he was writing.

'He came to New York,' said Woody, 'and rehearsed the band. This was a sensational thing for us. Of course, he had the patience of Job and to be perfectly candid we were out and out jazz players and some of us didn't read that well, but I don't think that was very important, because we could do other things.' Stravinsky recalled that he was obliged to copy the first of the three movements in quavers because the band couldn't read semi-quavers.

'He was completely intrigued with the band and said "Woody, you have a beautiful family!". No one will ever know what turned him on or what his reasoning was, because the piece was extremely subtle. It never really utilised the trumpets to any degree except with a certain amount of daintiness and lightness. I spent a lot of time with him socially later on and he explained to me that it had been a challenge for him to write for us. He had of course written Stravinsky and not jazz.'

Not wanting to upstage the jazz musicians, Stravinsky attended the first rehearsal dressed in his oldest polo-necked sweater and slacks. The jazz musicians on the other hand had shown their respect by dressing in their best suits!

Herman did a fine job in the difficult virtuoso clarinet role created for him. The impact of working with Stravinsky at close quarters moved the musicians very deeply, particularly arrangers Burns and Rogers. Stravinsky rehearsed the band again when it came to Hollywood. Shorty must have impressed the great man, for later he attended some concerts Shorty gave and is on record as saying 'I can listen to Shorty Rogers' good style with its dotted tradition, for stretches of fifteen minutes and more and not feel the time at all, whereas the weight of every "serious" virtuoso I know depressed me beyond the counter action of equanil in about five.' Shorty was to return the compliment by writing *Igor* for the Woodchoppers.

Now Neal Hefti and his wife Frances Wayne left the band to settle in Hollywood and Conrad Gozzo, one of the most powerful lead trumpeters ever, and Marky Markowitz joined Berman, Rogers and Candoli in the trumpets. Dave Tough succumbed finally to his illness and left in late September 1945. Generally regarded as irreplaceable, it seemed that the band must inevitably drop down a notch without him. Woody's good fortune held and he took on Don Lamond, a man who was and is dedicated to jazz and who was to prove to be outstanding amongst drummers and in his more modern way as good as Tough. He had Davey's respect for the roots, but he also had a more wide ranging awareness of contemporary jazz. His legion of discs with Woody are his testimonial, but he went on later to grace many splendid sessions, notably the ones for the Argo label by Chubby Jackson's big band with Bill Harris.

In 1938 the Benny Goodman orchestra gained a lot of prestige when it gave a concert in New York's until then exclusively symphony Carnegie Hall. Duke Ellington followed him to the hall in the early forties, and it seemed a natural place for the burgeoning Herd.

A concert was set for 25 March 1946 and it was decided to give *Ebony Concerto* its première. Ralph Burns had written an extended suite the previous summer while staying at Chubby Jackson's home in Long Island, and that also was to receive its première. Called *Summer Sequence*, it was a masterwork, full of beautiful melody and superb scoring, after the manner of but not derivative from Duke Ellington. At this stage it was in three parts, but later Burns was to compose an even more voluptuous fourth movement which became known as 'Early Autumn'. Unfortunately Stravinsky was engaged elsewhere, so the task of conducting his work fell to Walter Hendl.

The concert was sold out. Fortunately all of it except the concerto, *Summer Sequence* and five other numbers was recorded and issued later. Although the sound quality is far from perfect, the music is some of the most exciting ever caught on record. Classics abound. Bill Harris created exquisite versions of his ballads, *Mean To Me* and *Everywhere,* Flip Phillips had *Sweet And Lovely* to perfection and Red Norvo was dazzling on his two numbers, *I Surrender Dear* and *The Man I Love,* the rhythm section rode *Four Men On A Horse* and Pete Candoli popped buttons off his shirt with *Superman With A Horn* (in some less dignified performances of this latter Pete had swung to the stage from the balcony on a rope dressed in a Superman outfit).

The band, powered particularly by Harris and Lamond, exploded classic performances of *Bijou, Your Father's Moustache, Wild Root, The Good Earth, Blowing Up A Storm* and a delectable blues feature for Woody and Bill, *Panacea.*

Down Beat, after some obligatory carping about detail, noted that Herman ended both *Red Top* and the concluding *Wild Root* with 'a good four feet leap in the air'. Leaping in the air (and spinning his bass the while) was one of Chubby's specialities, and the leap was often emulated by the young but large Sonny Berman, who was a disciple of Chubby's. Sonny too was pretty hefty and on one occasion leapt and crashed through the stage to the next floor.

Copious *Down Beat* coverage left no doubt that the men were stars, and here were the seeds of trouble for later in the year.

The bulk of the programme was repeated in succeeding appearances in Baltimore and Boston, but not surprisingly the charismatic atmosphere of Carnegie was apparently not recaptured.

There then occurred a remarkable recording session in Chicago, or rather two sessions on 16 and 20 May 1946. These were by the Woodchoppers with Berman and Rogers on trumpet, Harris on trombone, Woody and Flip, and on piano Jimmy Rowles, who had replaced Tony Aless a month earlier. Chubby and guitarist Billy Bauer, about to leave the band, were also in the rhythm section with Lamond.

Shorty wrote *Steps, Igor* and *Nero's Conception,* Bauer contributed *Pam* and Flip composed *Lost Weekend. Fan It,* a survivor from the Isham Jones days, reappeared. The music was superb, with Berman having his last grand exposure on record. (When the author visited Shorty Rogers at his California home, the trumpeter brought out his most prized possessions, one of Sonny's mutes and a signed photograph of Igor Stravinsky.) Woody paid tributes to both Jimmy Noone with the trills on *Nero's Conception* and to Barney Bigard on *Steps,* despite the fact that the settings Rogers had created were amongst the most modern the musicians had experienced. The sessions were unique, and since this is the last time that he will be mentioned here and because his solos are so much to be cherished, let us summarize the bulk of the Sonny Berman solos on records: *Sidewalks Of Cuba, Your Father's Moustache, I Wonder, A Kiss Goodnight, Uncle*

Remus Said, Don't Worry 'Bout That Mule, Let It Snow, and *Someday Sweetheart* by the Woodchoppers of 12 October 1946. His solos on Ralph Burns's excellent arrangement of *Sidewalks Of Cuba* and on the V Disc *Don't Worry 'Bout That Mule* are especially outstanding and although the trumpet work on the version of the latter on Fanfare 43-143 is credited to Candoli, it is actually Sonny at his best.

The band grossed three quarters of a million dollars in 1946.

In September they recorded another lengthy Burns suite, *Lady McGowan's Dream*. This had typically imaginative Burns mood creating, adorned with solos from Woody, Shorty and Flip. Its antecedents are interesting. When the band was resident at the Panther Room of the Sherman Hotel in Chicago, a woman by the name of Lady McGowan checked into a suite and several other rooms. The hotel regarded her as some kind of visiting dignitary. Nobody knew her, but she was evidently a Woody fan and came every night to listen. One night she threw a big party for the band in her suite and caviar and champagne were laid on. A day or so later the management decided to check up on who she was and when they did they discovered that there was no such person as Lady McGowan. She had run up a tab of $4000 and when it was investigated her luggage turned out to be empty trunks. She had played hostess to the band at a splendid party and gone, to be immortalised in Burns's composition.

On 19 August when the band was resident at the massive Casino Gardens in Ocean Park, California, it travelled to Los Angeles where Stravinsky conducted the concerto in the recording studio. On 19 September in the same studio Ralph Burns played piano when the first three parts of *Summer Sequence* were recorded. Woody recalled that the studio seemed to be fur-lined, but later doctoring by the engineers made the discs acceptable. Burns had introduced a new and highly developed idiom to jazz with this suite, and the strength of form and lack of wasteful adornment are to be praised. Although it is the writing that grips the attention, the soloists were Chuck Wayne (Bauer's replacement and a Czech émigré whose real name is Jagelski), Harris and Sam Rubinwitch on baritone. It seems coincidental that Rubinwitch in the up tempo passage takes on a Harry Carney sound and Woody does his Bigard. The suite is perhaps Burns's ultimate achievement in jazz, and ranks with Eddie Sauter's 'Focus' suite (for Stan Getz) as a serious and successful attempt at a new form of jazz expression.

Two days later, under the titles of the Sonny Berman Big Eight and the Bill Harris Big Eight, Burns joined Berman, Harris, Phillips Lamond and others to record the classic non-Herman tracks that included Burns's exquisite *Nocturne*. The baritone player on the date was Serge Chaloff, who was to be one of the leading lights of the Second Herd.

In December *The Blues Are Brewin'* from the film 'New Orleans' in which the band had appeared briefly was recorded, along with two of Mr. Bishop's aces restored from the old days, *Blue Flame* and *Woodchopper's Ball*.

The band was at the top, but the departure of Chubby Jackson and Billy Bauer had been symptomatic. There was unrest in the ranks as the stars decided that they should be paid more or that they should go where they would be paid more. That month, after the band played a dance at the University of Indiana, Woody told the musicians that the band was folding. Many different people have offered different reasons for the break up, but Woody later stated unequivocally that it was because of illness in his immediate family.

As George Simon has noted, the great big band era finished that month, as Benny Goodman, Tommy Dorsey, Harry James, Les Brown, Jack Teagarden and Benny Carter all broke up their bands. But let it be said that many of them were to reform later.

Including Woody Herman's.

Chapter Four

The First Herd, on two weeks' notice in December 1946, was at the close one of the highest paid bands there had been. Herman, always an intelligent and perceptive man, knew that the band had reached the top and that it couldn't better itself. He had recently bought the beautiful Hollywood home that had belonged to Humphrey Bogart and Lauren Bacall, and he wanted to spend more time with Charlotte and his daughter Ingrid (Woody and Ingrid still live in the same house). He walked away from the band business and had his longest holiday from band leading. It lasted seven months.

But he didn't stop working because he recorded as a vocalist with studio groups and worked on a radio series with Peggy Lee and her husband Dave Barbour's orchestra called 'The Electric Hour'.

An old friend of Woody's, Al Jarvis, had a local radio station and he suggested that Woody should present a two or three hour disc jockey show each Saturday morning, mainly with the idea of giving him something to do. The programme was totally informal and unscripted. Woody just went on the air and started talking. When the word got round friends from all over Hollywood began turning up, and Woody brought them onto the air, so that in addition to Woody there were many high powered guests of the calibre of Johnny Mercer. Where other stations struggled to get such eminent attractions, the 'eminent attractions' used to turn up for Woody without even being invited. Herman was having a ball, but it was too good to last, and there was much resentment amongst other California disc jockeys that a musician should trample so heavily in their preserve.

Stan Getz. Photo David Redfern

One result was the formation of the first disc jockeys' union. Another, the clincher, was that a couple of the more outraged stations refused to play any of Woody's records; so he thanked Al and left.

Woody had worked all his life and now, with his beautiful new home to enjoy, he was able to spend his time lying around in the sun. He didn't like it at all.

High taxes on bands and the advent of television were two power-ful items that caused the mayhem of December 1946. Although most of the bands returned in one shape or another, it had to be faced that big band music was no longer the nation's pop music and the hysteria and 'star' status had gone forever. Woody's next band, the Second Herd, was to be his most musical to date. Its appeal was to be much more cerebral than that of the earlier band. The listening public wasn't ready for the bebop derived sounds, and while he has no regrets because in terms of jazz history the Second Herd was vitally important, the heady days of financial success with the First Herd were not to be repeated. 'I must be candid and honest by saying that I lost a barrel of money with that 1948-9 band,' said Woody.

The story goes that Woody heard a superb performance by the black trumpeter Ernie Royal, and wanted to hire him and then remembered he hadn't got a band to put him in. Whatever the reason, the band bug had got Woody once more, and by the middle of 1947 he was itching to go again. There was a band working in the Spanish section of Los Angeles that was led by a trumpeter called Tommy di Carlo and it had an unusual line up of trumpet, four tenors and rhythm. It used arrangements by the extraordinarily talented Gene Roland and saxophonist Jimmy Giuffre. Woody de-cided to hire three of the tenors and to commission Giuffre to create some arrangements for his new band. The three men he hired were Stan Getz, Zoot Sims, and Herbie Steward, the latter being a par-ticular asset in that he doubled alto and tenor saxes. It remains unclear why Woody didn't ask Roland to write for him, Gene was later to produce some of the best composition ever done for the Stan Kenton band. Getz, Sims and Steward were all primarily motivated by the playing of Lester Young, and they had drenched the Young sound in the improvisational methods of Parker and Gillespie. Getz and Sims particularly were themselves to become jazz influences, and it has been argued that some of the later incumbents of Woody's tenor chairs, men like Richie Kamuca, Bill Perkins, Jerry Coker and

Zoot Sims. Photo Polydor

Dick Hafer, were in fact influenced by Parker and Young only through what they heard in the distilled version of the Parker/Young styles in the playing of Getz and Sims.

Most of the men in the new band were young, but there were some familiar faces. Shorty Rogers had left the First Herd to fulfil the dream he and his wife had of living in California. They bought a little house in Burbank. 'Nothing was happening. I literally couldn't even pick the 'phone up and call anyone. I didn't know anyone to call! Eventually I got a little work with a band led by Butch Stone that had Stan Getz and Herbie Steward in it, and as soon as they let me know that Woody was re-forming, I was back!' Section mate Marky Markowitz returned with Shorty as did lead alto Sam Marowitz. Don Lamond came back and Walt Yoder, who went back as far as Woody's days with Isham Jones, came in on bass. Another bass player from the Band That Plays The Blues who had replaced Yoder in 1943, Gene Sargent, joined to play guitar. Ralph Burns returned as writer in chief, and the new men included the fine trombonist Earl Swope, pianist Fred Otis and a major new jazz voice,

55

the baritone from Boston, Serge Chaloff. Chaloff had been with the bands of George Auld, Jimmy Dorsey and Boyd Raeburn. Originally influenced by Harry Carney, he was quicker than most of the youngsters to realise the significance of Charlie Parker's playing, and by the time the Second Herd got going, Chaloff had completed the absorption of Parker's style and its transfer to the baritone. He was undoubtedly one of the finest players of the instrument, and alas like a nucleus of men in the new band, he fell victim to heroin addiction.

The problem of drug addiction was a major one with this band. Nowadays the tragedy is a commonplace amongst young people the world over. Then it was less prevalent but unfortunately of high incidence amongst young modern jazz musicians. Herman, like Duke Ellington, was sympathetic as far as he could be, and uninvolved. If people could work in his band without their addiction influencing their performances, he was prepared to respect their private lives as just that. Fortunately most of those in the band who were addicts cured themselves completely later on, and went on to lead useful and happy lives. This is surely an example to give hope to others, but while drug addiction was dominant it made things almost impossible for Woody.

In retrospect, Woody told *Down Beat* what it had been like. In 1950 he had cut down to a small group of reliable men. 'You can't imagine how good it feels to look at this group and find them all awake, to play a set and not have someone conk out in the middle of a chorus.' Herman had chased 'connections' out of jazz clubs across America, but, once there was a nucleus of addicts in the band, he had tremendous difficulties. 'They have to have company, and one in the band is enough to get it started. These guys are young, easily influenced. Once they're on it, there's not much you can do. There were some serious things Ralph Burns had written that I was very interested in. We tried rehearsing them but had to call if off. The guys would sit around and talk about them, but they just didn't have enough energy to play.'

On the lighter side, Serge Chaloff seems to have been a character. Terry Gibbs remembered him as the greatest liar in the world. 'He would fall asleep and his cigarettes would burn holes three feet long in hotel mattresses. But when the hotel manager confronted him with the burnt mattresses he would say "How dare you talk to me like that. I happen to be the *Down Beat* and *Metronome* poll winner. How dare you even suggest that I . . ." Finally the manager would wind up on his hands and knees apologising. Once Serge put a telephone book up against his hotel room door and decided to get in some target pistol practice. He shot through the book, or around the book, and into the door. So the manager accused him of this. Serge tried to lie his way out. He couldn't. The manager told him "You'll pay $24 for that door or you'll go to jail." When we left Serge insisted that, having paid for it, it was his door. I helped him to drag it down to the band bus!'

Never slow to take advantage of an asset, Woody let Chaloff take a good proportion of the band's solo space, and indeed his horn was featured more than any baritone has ever been featured with any big band outside Gerry Mulligan's.

But unfortunately, in behaviour characteristic of a heroin addict, Serge was instrumental in introducing some of the other men to his habit. Eventually, despite the brilliance of his jazz playing, Woody decided that Serge had to go. Since he came from Boston, Woody decided that he should leave when the band next visited the area. He told Serge in advance, and Serge was distraught since he depended on his income to finance his habit. The break was to be made at a famous dance hall near Boston, Nutter's On The Charles, a picturesque building backing onto the River Charles.

At the intermission on the fateful night Serge called Woody over to a window overlooking the river. 'Look out there, Woody. What do you see?' Herman peered through the window. 'A lot of water,' he said. 'Look more closely,' said Serge. 'Well,' said Woody, 'there's some litter floating about.'

'That litter,' said Serge, 'is the band's baritone book. Now you can't fire me, because I'm the only person in the world that knows the book by heart.'

It took Woody another six months before he was able to unload Chaloff from his band.

The other main soloists were to be the tenors, mainly Getz and Sims, but later on most potently, Al Cohn, who also wrote some magnificent charts for the Herd. Cohn replaced Herbie Steward in January 1948. The three men, all with roots in Lester Young's style, had completely different ways of improvising. It is an understatement to say that Getz was able to create music of breathtaking beauty. He could swing, too, but not as convincingly as John Haley

Al Cohn. Photo Jazz Journal International

Sims. Both were by this time mature and inventive players of the first order, but because of this the greatness of Cohn's work has been overlooked. Lou Levy, who was to join some months later, in September, told the author 'Al was the biggest influence on me in that band. I'd never heard anyone play that way. He's really a gem, in fact I think you'll find that he's Stan Getz's favourite player. The band was so vital and clean and it had so much energy. And I've never heard a band sound as polished and yet so original.'

Shorty Rogers was the man who introduced the tune *Four Brothers*. 'Jimmy Giuffre had written it out and had it copied, but for some reason he couldn't go to the rehearsal so he gave it to me and I took it. That was the first time it was played.'

Four Brothers, written by Giuffre on the chords of *Jeepers Creepers* and titled by Woody, was to become as much part of Herman lore as *Woodchopper's Ball* and has been a nightly feature ever since. With Petrillo's recording ban looming at the end of 1947, Woody rushed the new band into the recording studios, and during December history was made again. Unfortunately, there was more trouble with the quality of the studios, and many of the sides the band made had to have echo added before they were acceptable. *Four Brothers* featured the four saxes including Herbie Steward (Cohn had not yet joined) along with a dash of Woody's clarinet. The solos were in the bop idiom and, apart from the freshness of the horns, the piece was notable for the brilliance of Lamond's drumming. He was to be every bit as important to this band as Tough had initially been to the First Herd; it is not only Buddy Rich who feels that Lamond has been the greatest big band drummer in jazz.

Other interesting tracks that December were Shorty's composition *Keen And Peachy*, a reworking of *Fine And Dandy* featuring the saxophones and trombonist Earl Swope, Cohn's fine arrangement of *The Goof And I,* and a splendid blues, *I've Got News For You*. Woody sang the amusing lyrics, Shorty wrote the arrangement and soloed, and the sax section played a transcription of Charlie Parker's alto solo from his version of *Dark Shadows*. This passage was the inspiration for reed man Med Flory to form his Supersax band in later years. *News* concluded with a typically powerful solo from Ernie Royal, very much the spark plug of the band in the way that Pete Candoli had been earlier.

Ralph Burns had written a final movement to *Summer Sequence* and the band now recorded it as *Early Autumn*. It is a beautiful composition and after Woody's alto there are eight sublime bars of Getz's tenor and a coda written for the saxes in Giuffre's Four Brothers style. Almost a year later to the day the band recorded the piece again for Capitol featuring vibist Terry Gibbs and an extended solo from Getz. Both versions are classic jazz performances.

Mary Ann McCall rejoined Woody on December 22. She was easily the most jazz orientated girl singer that he ever had, and good though her records are, it seems she was never able to record at her best. Happily many of the broadcasts made by the Second Herd survive, and she is better represented on these. She was a warm singer and her style was very popular with the musicians in the band. Cohn and guitarist Jimmy Raney joined in January, and again we have to go to the broadcasts to hear how effective Al's tenor was, because he doesn't solo on any of the studio recordings — there can never have been another band with such a plethora of tenor soloists.

In early February the band began a residence at the Hollywood Palladium that was crucial to its career. It made almost nightly broadcasts, and this was vital, since it was going to be the end of the year before it would record officially. Many of the broadcasts survive in varying sound quality and they include most of the exciting repertoire.

May found the band working at the Capitol Theatre in New York with a new, or not so new trombonist, Bill Harris, and in July another member of the old firm came back, Chubby Jackson. In late 1947 Chubby had gone to Europe with a fine band that he called his Fifth Dimensional Jazz Group. Lou Levy was a member.

'I came into the Second Herd through the back door,' said Lou. 'Tiny Kahn was my great mentor, and he got me a job in Chubby's marvellous band. Chubby had used George Wallington, but George fell sick just before they were about to leave for Sweden. When Chubby came back he went with Woody, and a couple of months later he got me in, to replace Ralph Burns, who wasn't leaving but was concentrating on writing. That was the beginning of the whole ball of wax. I stayed with that band until it broke up.'

Jackson resumed his role of cheer leader and encourager of young musicians, and it was as if he had never been away. Coupled with Lamond and Harris, he made up a powerful influence in the band.

When Jimmy Raney left in September, Woody decided to bring

the vibraphone back into the line up, and the remarkable Terry Gibbs joined. Gibbs remains one of the hardest swinging players of the instrument, and his solos light up many of the broadcasts from the period. It is notable that the emphasis at this time was more heavily on the soloists than perhaps at any other time, and some of the performances were extended.

The apex of the band's achievement seems to have been during its residence at the Royal Roost Club in New York. This lasted for one month from October 24. On the opening night Dizzy Gillespie, Stan Kenton and most of the men from their bands were in the audience, and this seems to have given the Herd a momentum that lasted throughout the month. Certainly the extracts from radio broadcasts which survive from this month show the band at its best. They include such unique performances as an eight minute version of Shorty Rogers' *Boomsie* (later recorded as *That's Right*) that crowded in solos from Gibbs, Chaloff, Levy, Swope, Royal, Getz, Harris and Herman all on peak form. And *Yucca,* the only arrangement ever written by Zoot Sims (it took him six months to write).

This was a particularly good time for Mary Ann McCall. Until now her best recorded performance had been *Wrap Your Troubles In Dreams* with the later First Herd, but now, with Woody giving her plenty to sing, she excelled herself. Her style had elements of Kay Starr's early jazz singing days, and also touches of Anita O'Day, but she phrased and attacked like an instrumentalist. She had vocal competition from a small group within the band which used Chubby Jackson and Shorty Rogers and Terry Gibbs to sing bebop scat on classics of culture like *We The People Bop* and *Lemon Drop.* Shorty Rogers, Stan Getz, Terry Gibbs and the rhythm section comprised the Pirates, a small group featured within the band, but one that also recorded with great success for the Prestige label.

The band made at least eleven full scale broadcasts from the Royal Roost, and as has been mentioned not the least important item was the fact that they included solos by Al Cohn, not represented on the commercial issues. The fine trumpeter Red Rodney came into the band at the Roost as a replacement for Marky Markowitz. Don Lamond is also heard to tremendous effect here — of the opening night at the Roost *Down Beat's* Mike Levin wrote 'the standout attraction by far was the superlative drumming of ex-Washingtonian Don Lamond'.

Don Lamond. Photo Jazz Journal International

Artistically triumphant, the Herd was not pulling big crowds and the booking fees it received were way down from the First Herd days. From the Roost it returned to Los Angeles to work at the Empire Room for Gene Norman. In an attempt to pull in a young audience a special part of the room was partitioned off as a no drink area, and each Saturday there was an hour when no drinks at all were served. It worked at first. The room held 600 people and on the first night 500 were turned away. Despite more broadcasts, business tailed off.

At the end of the year union boss James C. Petrillo lifted his ban on musicians making commercial recordings. Woody signed for Capitol and immediately began recording for them. Again the tide was taken at the flood and the on form Herd recorded *That's Right*, a variation on *I've Found A New Baby* called *Keeper Of The Flame, Lemon Drop* and the successful reworking of *Early Autumn* to feature Getz and Gibbs. Mary Ann sang Duke's *I Got It Bad*, and Woody sang Shorty's *I Ain't Gonna Wait Too Long* with solos from Bill Harris and Ernie Royal. Getz's sensual playing on *Early Autumn* was a triumphant success and earned him the nickname 'The Sound'.

In January 1949 Chubby Jackson, recently married, decided to quit the road, and his eventual replacement was the stormy and talented Oscar Pettiford, one of the most gifted bassists and writers jazz music has produced. Zoot Sims left to join Buddy Rich's band and Woody took Jimmy Giuffre from the Jimmy Dorsey band, so that Giuffre finally was able to play his own composition, *Four Brothers*!

During the year Woody played a number of concerts with Nat Cole and the series was very successful. In February the package appeared at Carnegie Hall, and predictably the sense of occasion generated by the First Herd's appearance there was not recaptured. A couple of days later the band made its first television appearance in the unlikely setting of the Eddie Condon Show. 'We're boppin' ourselves silly tonight!' was Condon's comment.

A crucial blow came in March when Lamond left to join Harry James. The replacements, first Shadow Wilson and then Shelly Manne, were good, but unable to take over from Lamond in the way he had done from Tough. Then in April Stan Getz and Al Cohn finally left with their chairs being given to Gene Ammons and Buddy Savitt. Ammons, son of the famous pianist, was already well known as an aggressive hard blowing soloist, but he adopted the established role with Woody, and played with a smoothness that surprised everybody. His most notable features with the band were on *More Moon* and *Not Really The Blues* done for Capitol. Savitt took on the difficult job of featured tenor in *Early Autumn,* and the two worked a duet spot into *Lemon Drop* with Savitt's Wardell Gray-inspired playing a good foil for the bustling Ammons. The band was still reworking First Herd hits like *Apple Honey* and *Wild Root* to good effect, but new material like Johnny Mandel's arrangement of *Not Really The Blues,* a sixteen bar stomper was also coming into the book (this one was a favourite of the band's if Woody had left the stand, and on such occasions it would rampage for many minutes).

Joe Mondragon came in as a replacement for Oscar Pettiford in July. Oscar had broken his arm in a game of softball. Joe, who had replaced Chubby in the First Herd, did not stay long and was in turn replaced by Mert Oliver. Ernie Royal, a key figure in the band, decided to leave to form his own group and in September a stern economic situation forced Woody to ask the band to take a cut in salary. Terry Gibbs refused to accept this and left. Incredibly Woody was able to replace him with Milt Jackson for less money. At the same time Gene Ammons went and Billy Mitchell, later to make a name with Gillespie and Basie, took over, but in turn was soon superseded by Don Lanphere, a brilliant creative jazz soloist who had recorded some classic sides with trumpeter Fats Navarro. The band returned to Carnegie Hall with Nat Cole in November and then moved to the Paramount Theatre. Unfortunately at this period, its closing moments, it did not record, and consequently we have no record of how Jackson and Mitchell sounded within its ranks.

Despite the fact that 14 appearances with Nat Cole had made a profit of about $77,000, the tremendous costs of running the band began to drag it down and it played its last engagement in the Municipal Auditorium of Oklahoma City on 4 December. Woody estimated that over its two year life he lost $180,000.

Artistically extremely successful, the sound that the Second Herd evolved was to remain an ingredient in each of Woody's bands that followed. Ironically, after it folded, *Down Beat* announced that it had been chosen as the best band in the magazine's Readers' Poll. The Herd had been given 1,042 votes. Duke Ellington was second with 301 and Charlie Barnet third with 249.

On 6 December Woody opened at the Tropicana in Havana with a small group which included Bill Harris, Milt Jackson, Ralph Burns,

Red Mitchell and Shelly Manne. They played there for four weeks and then returned home.

Considering the comparatively small number of titles recorded for Capitol, it is fortunate that so many broadcasts by the Second Herd survived to appear on record. Apart from the Royal Roost airchecks, there are fine collections from the band's stay at the Hollywood Palladium in February and March 1948 and from various broadcasts from the Empire Room, New York's Commodore Hotel and from the Marine Ballroom in Atlantic City.

Chapter Five

'There's no doubt the band business is coming back,' Woody told *Down Beat* in November 1950. He completed his contract with Capitol that year, producing only two notable jazz titles, Al Cohn's *Music To Dance To* and a track featuring Bill Harris, tenorist Bob Graf and Woody, Sonny Berman's tune *Sonny Speaks*, which Sonny had originally titled *They Went Thataway*.

'The public is dance conscious now,' continued Woody, and his next bands were to try to cater for that kind of audience. He signed a new contract with MGM Records which was to produce his least inspired period of recordings. It began pleasantly enough with Woody and a studio band backing singer Billy Eckstine on four titles arranged by Pete Rugolo. But the fine new band that Woody had shaped during 1950 and 1951 was restricted to insipid and novelty arrangements. There were the odd moments of excitement when tenorist Kenny Pinson soloed on *Leo The Lion*, a Tiny Kahn chart that also featured another fine soloist, a young trombonist called Urbie Green. Again Woody's band was to be an incubator for young talents, and at this period its ranks included tenorists Bill Perkins and Phil Urso, trumpeters Don Fagerquist and Doug Mettome (two of the most sadly undervalued practitioners of the horn), and the great pianist Dave McKenna. Sonny Igoe was another good drummer in the tradition.

Because of the fragile nature of the band business at the time this Herd remained cautious and unadventurous in the recording studio. But there is one glorious example of it in full cry. In August 1951 it played a date in Kansas City. Charlie Parker, who had come home to visit his mother, came along to the date and was persuaded to sit in. Happily the trombonist Urbie Green recorded the proceedings on a domestic tape recorder. With no charts designed to feature Parker, the Herd played its normal programme and Parker took all the solo space — *Four Brothers* has to be heard to be believed!

America's involvement in the Korean war began to affect the bands, and Dave McKenna was drafted and sent to Korea as a cook. Nat Pierce, a splendid musician who was to have a lasting influence in succeeding Herman Herds, began the first of his ten years with Woody. Nat had run his own bands in Boston where he grew up with musicians like Ruby Braff and worked with giants like Charlie Parker. In those days his piano playing was deeply involved with bebop and his bands of the time reflected the turbulent music. He digested and absorbed all the aspects of contemporary jazz, but eventually emerged as a brilliant middle of the road player who in turn deputised for men as distinguished as Count Basie and Stan Kenton. He became a friend of Duke Ellington's, and on one occasion Duke asked him to sit in with the Ellington band. 'When I was young,' Duke told the audience, 'my piano teacher Miss Clinkscales gave me some very good advice. "Don't ever," she told me, "come up in back of Nat Pierce".'

Nat told the author 'I first joined Woody in 1951 at Hershey Park, Pennsylvania. Some of the fellows from my Boston band were now with him, and they recommended me to him when Dave had to leave. He called me on the 'phone and I went and that was that. It was one of the high points in my life, because although I'd played with a lot of the great jazz musicians, I had never been part of an actual big time jazz band. We had Bill Perkins, Dick Hafer, Urbie and his brother Jack Green, Carl Fontana and Arno Marsh in the band. Ralph Burns was the top arranger at that time. Some of the guys in the band had written some things and I wrote a dance medley, but it wasn't my turn yet. The way it worked with Woody, and it still works like that today, is that a guy comes into the band shouting "I can write, I can write!" and nobody ever asks him anything, so he writes an arrangement on his own. Then, after a few rejected arrangements you say well, forget it. And then maybe six months later Woody asks you to write an arrangement!

'Woody wasn't happy with MGM. What do you do if a record

company won't record what you want to play? You form your own record company, and Woody did just that with a guy called Howard Richman. They called the label Mars and we recorded for it from 1952 to 1954.'

The music that the band played was very polished, but it also had the inspired spirit of every Herman band, and the Mars recordings brought the jazz fans roaring back. Ralph Burns created an original invention in *Stompin' At The Savoy*, which featured Woody and tenorist Arno Marsh. He also wrote the more complex *Teressita*, a beautiful melody to feature Woody's alto and Pierce on piano ('I had to practice that one at home!' said Nat). Pierce and Chubby Jackson wrote the chart of *Blue Lou* between them. 'Chubby sang it to me and I wrote it down, and Ralph Burns and I wrote the arrangement of *Perdido*. I did *Wooftie* and Ralph did *Men From Mars*, those were two of the stomp pieces. I remember the sessions because Carl Fontana was fairly new in the band. When we did the vocal piece *Jump In The Line* he was required to play a little trombone break. When it came he froze at the mike and we had to do another take. It wouldn't happen today, because he's one of the greatest in the world.'

Woody dug out a Jimmy Giuffre piece called *Quart Of Bones* and decided to retitle it *Four Others*. By now Jerry Coker, later to be a highly respected music teacher, had replaced Arno Marsh and trumpeters Bernie Glow and Ernie Royal plus trombonist Kai Winding were added to the section pending the arrival of permanent replacements. The result was a marvellous shout up for the trombone section with solos by Winding, Vern Friley, Frank Rehak and Urbie Green.

The band was booked for its first European tour in April 1954. The last job in New York before flying to Oslo was at the Basin Street on 29 March. But Woody made another gig before leaving. On 31 March an old friend of his, trumpeter Buck Clayton, was recording a jam session for Columbia. Producer George Avakian suggested that Woody might come along and bring his clarinet. Unfortunately the Chopper's clarinet had already been packed by the band boy and was stowed in the luggage at Idlewild Airport ready for the flight. The band boy rushed over there in a cab and with special permission rooted out the horn and dashed back to Columbia with it. Working with Buck, Urbie, Trummy Young, Al Cohn, Walter Page, Jo Jones and the others in that jam session, Woody produced some of his finest clarinet playing ever. He soared over the band on *How Hi The Fi* and partnered Buck in some filigree improvisations on *Blue Moon*, amongst others.

The European trip was a colossal success with most concerts sold out. One of Nat Pierce's pals, the great trumpet soloist Dick Collins, was complemented by high note men Bill Castagnino and Al Porcino in the trumpets. Dick Kenney and Keith Moon were joined in the trombones by bass trumpeter Cy Touff, an agile performer on his cumbersome instrument and one of the main brass soloists. The tenors were Perkins, Coker and Dick Hafer, and Jack 'The Admiral' Nimitz was on baritone, while Pierce led the great rhythm section with Red Kelly on bass and Chuck Flores at the drums. Some of the sidemen recorded imaginative sessions in Paris with Henri Renaud and Ralph Burns, who was on the tour to play the piano role in *Summer Sequence*. The simian thinking of the British Musicians' Union had persuaded it to ban appearances by American musicians within the realm, and the *Melody Maker* resourcefully arranged two concerts by the band in Dublin, the Irish capital. They laid on flights from Britain and on Sunday 2 May, a veritable air lift of jazz fans arrived in Ireland. They were not disappointed. *Perdido, Early Autumn, Four Brothers* — the band played its heart out for them. And a man already a big favourite with the European audience, Bill Perkins, established his tradition of tenor ballad playing with *These Foolish Things* (Bill later returned to Dublin when he was with Stan Kenton and that band had to subvert the Union's machinations).

That May Woody recorded three fine tracks for Columbia, *Blame Boehm, Mulligan Tawny* and *The Third Herd*, and also cut a vocal album for the same label with the Erroll Garner Trio in July, but September saw him back with Capitol. By now Nat Pierce's writing was exerting an influence alongside Ralph Burns's, and the band recorded his arrangements of *Boo Hoo* and *Sleep* in those first sessions. Burns excelled with brilliant arrangements of two features for Bill Perkins, *Misty Morning* and *Ill Wind*, the latter also including a delicious trumpet solo from Dick Collins. Ralph's more robust *Autobahn Blues* featured Nat, Woody, Perkins and trumpeter John Howell. The long playing medium allowed for a six minute version of *Apple Honey* with wailing tenor from Perkins and Hafer, whilst Cy Touff rooted in the undergrowth for truffles. This was a polished and now classic Herd.

Woodchopper's Ball was done for Capitol with the then popular mambo rhythm and the riff from *Jumpin' With Symphony Sid* which was to remain an integral part of it. The personnel remained fairly stable except for two important changes which brought in the fine tenor player Richie Kamuca to replace Hafer and bassist John Beal for Kelly. Bill Perkins left to join Kenton and was replaced by Art Pirie.

On 6 and 7 June 1955 the Herd recorded fourteen titles for Capitol, several of which were magnificent and remain fresh sounding to this day. Nat Pierce loved the music of Horace Silver and the first of his reworkings of Horace's music was *Opus De Funk*, which swung irresistibly for five minutes, with notable solos from Kamuca, Collins, Touff and Herman. Manny Albam contributed *Captain Ahab* in the powerhouse stomp Herman tradition, and again Kamuca excelled. Nat Pierce tidied up a head arrangement of *Sentimental Journey* piling up the riffs towards the end as he had done on *Opus De Funk*, and Keith Moon contributed some incisive wa-wa muted trombone. Woody wrote *I Remember Duke* in an Ellington vein and once again Moon's trombone was relevant. This was a time when drum features were popular and the magnificent Chuck Flores essayed *Skinned*, *Skinned Again* and at a later session, *Drums In Hi-Fly* brought Buddy Rich back into the band for the first time since *Your Father's Moustache*, recorded almost ten years to the day before. But the Rich feature was done by a mixture of session men and Herdsmen, because Woody broke the band up in September 1955. The reason was a lucrative offer from the Riviera Hotel in Las Vegas for him to play there with a smaller group. He cut down to an eight piece band keeping Dick Collins and Johnny Coppola on trumpets, Touff on bass trumpet, Kamuca on tenor and Flores on drums. Monty Budwig joined on bass and Norman Pockrandt came in briefly on piano before Vince Guaraldi took over. On 1 December Woody brought the group over to the Capitol Studios in Hollywood and recorded eight delightful tracks for an album including *Bags' Other Grove*, Coppola's wailing variation on Milt Jackson's blues. Woody played a beautiful lower register solo which harked back to Bigard and Noone again.

When the engagement at the Riviera finished Woody built up a big band again, and this time Bill Harris returned to the trombones with Bobby Lamb and Wayne Andre. Arno Marsh was alongside Kamuca for a recording session in Chicago in May 1956 and Vic Feldman was added on vibraphone for a potent series of blues numbers including *Trouble In Mind* and *Dupree Blues* from Woody's early days, as well as classics like *Pinetop's Blues* and *Call it Stormy Monday*. The Las Vegas octet had recorded *Basin Street Blues* and the Joe Williams hit *Every Day I Have The Blues* and these joined the rest in a classic album entitled 'Blues Groove'. Woody sang with great feeling, and there were potent eruptions from Harris, notably in the one instrumental, *Blues Groove*, a swinging Coppola riff pattern which in later Herds changed its name to *Cousins*. Although he had left the band by then, Nat Pierce sent in the charts of *Trouble In Mind* and *Call it Stormy Monday*.

At the beginning of 1957 Woody decided to change labels and moved to Norman Granz's Verve company. The results were not outstanding. Initially Norman teamed Woody with excellent small groups including Harris, Charlie Shavers, Ben Webster and Jimmy Rowles and Woody confined himself to the vocals. By the summer of that year Willie Dennis had come into the band to sit alongside Lamb and Bill Harris and Bill Berry and Danny Styles had joined Coppola and Bill Castagnino in the trumpets. Jay Migliori was the main tenor soloist, but somehow the band was characterized by the rather cold playing of pianist John Bunch. The album they recorded for Verve had some good writing by Gene Roland and a couple of interesting features for Harris, but somehow the fire wasn't there the way it should have been. However, it was good to hear adventurers still in the band, and the ill starred Willie Dennis had some rare exposure and Bill Berry made his solo debut.

An exciting curiosity from this period and a minefield for historians was the music recorded at a dance which probably occurred in Los Angeles in early 1958. Certainly Bill Harris was on hand, for he buckets through some unmistakable rampaging solos, and tenorist Arno Marsh had returned once more. The eight tracks which survive from this occasion include *Natchel Blues* which has Woody in soulful vein before Harris unpacks the dynamite and a lovely *Body And Soul* with Woody on alto. Standard Herd mayhem includes the mambo *Woodchopper's Ball* and Pierce's arrangement of *Opus De Funk*. It seems likely that Pete Jolly is the pianist and this could be the remarkable Jake Hanna's first appearance on drums with Woody.

It seems unlikely that this was the regular Herd and since the setting was Los Angeles it could have been that Woody put the band together while spending some time at home. Later that year when he was down to a small group again he was invited to bring a big band to play on the first ever colour television broadcast. Comedian Jerry

Lewis had broken his partnership with Dean Martin, and had been given his own show for the colour debut in New York. Woody simply hired the band that Nat Pierce had in the town at the time. It sounded so good that it was decided to record it for the Everest label. Nat rooted round and found many obscure and invaluable arrangements that various people had written for earlier Herds (like Al Cohn's *I Cover The Waterfront,* Johnny Mandel's *Sinbad The Tailor* and Ralph Burns' *Fire Island).* This eminent band included Cohn, Sam Donahue and Paul Quinichette on tenors, Chubby Jackson, Billy Bauer and Don Lamond in the rhythm section with Nat, Bob Brookmeyer (because Harris was in Las Vegas), Frank Rehak and Billy Byers on trombones and a formidable trumpet section of Ernie Royal, Bernie Glow, Al Stewart, Nick Travis and Marky Markowitz. Woody was on tremendous form. Nat had done a marvellous job in shaping the arrangements and writing new bits where parts were lost. Everest was the first company to use the new 35 millimetre wide recording tape, and the results were excellent, with Woody in good voice for the only vocal, the inevitable *Caldonia.* Woody persuaded Bob Brookmeyer to tread the hallowed ground of *Bijou,* and there was a generally attractive distribution of solos throughout the session. The following week with Woody absent, what was virtually the same band came to Everest to record under Chubby's name. Woody returned to the same label with a studio group including latin expert Tito Puente to record some mambo tracks and, with an orthodox line up, yet another essay on *Woodchopper's Ball* along with a clutch of original charts. Everest was much more ambitious in commissioning a new recording of *Summer Sequence* and later one of *Ebony Concerto.* Guitarist Charlie Byrd had joined Woody as a featured soloist, and his classical style was featured in *Summer Sequence* and four sambas which together made up an album. Don Lamond returned for the *Ebony Concerto* session which was conducted by Elliott Lawrence, but neither performance of the major suites excelled the original Columbia versions.

The end of 1958 saw Woody down to a sextet with Nat Adderley on cornet, Eddie Costa doubling piano and vibraphone, Byrd on guitar, Keeter Betts bass, and Jimmy Campbell drums. The sextet recorded in January and February 1959, but the music was pleasant rather than profound.

The British Musicians' Union was moving into the twentieth

century and was permitting a controlled exchange of British and American musicians. Woody travelled to London with a nucleus of Adderley, Byrd, Betts, Campbell, pianist Guaraldi, lead trumpeter Reunald Jones and trombonist Bill Harris. There he rehearsed a big band with that nucleus and nine British musicians. The band rehearsed for a few days before its tour. Tenorist Don Rendell recalls 'We thought things were going quite well, and then quite suddenly Woody stopped us. He really hammered us. He used all kinds of phrases that I can't remember, but it was to the effect that the band didn't have enough balls in it.' Trombonist Eddie Harvey remembers that the British musicians hadn't grasped that Woody wanted them to play with about four times the volume that they had been doing. 'After the pep talk the effect was electric, just as though Woody had turned a switch, and the band immediately played better. From that moment we never looked back.' The Anglo American Herd was one of Woody's triumphs, and for the first time a British audience was blown out of its seats by the authentic Herman sound. Bill Harris was a sensation, soloing on *Playgirl Stroll* and the rambling, slow Gene Roland composition *Like Some Blues, Man, Like*. (Roland wrote under the pseudonym Ted Richards.)

Back in the States that summer, Nat Pierce organised a big band line up for some more recordings, this time for the SESAC label. Despite the presence of Red Rodney, Ernie Royal, Bob Brookmeyer, Frank Rehak, Al Cohn, Dick Hafer, Zoot Sims and Don Lamond, the results sounded anonymous, and didn't really have the Herman stamp. Perhaps this was because SESAC, a company which recorded music solely for use by radio stations, imposed heavy restrictions on the character of the music used. Recordings for the company by Count Basie and Duke Ellington were similarly afflicted.

Woody had another collection of stars under his name at the 1959 Monterey Festival, this time with vastly more success. Zoot Sims, Bill Perkins, Richie Kamuca and baritone man Med Flory were there to chomp through *Four Brothers* with drummer Mel Lewis powering them in a way that made one reflect on his possibilities as a Herdsman. *Like Some Blues, Man, Like* simmered again with splendid blues from Victor Feldman's vibes, Conte Candoli, Bill Perkins, Charlie Byrd, Woody, trumpeter Ray Linn and Urbie Green, who played a beautifully lyrical *Skylark*. Al Porcino reached for the sky after everyone else had done with *Apple Honey*. 'I wish I could take this band on the road,' said Woody, and one could well understand his feelings.

Tenorist Don Lanphere had been in that band and he was to be the outstanding soloist in the comparatively ordinary band of 1960 with a beautiful solo feature of *Darn That Dream* recorded for the Crown label in Chicago.

In the early sixties Nat Pierce began nagging at Woody to reform the big band on a permanent basis. Woody recorded an attractive album of clarinet solos backed by Nat with the fine bassist Chuck Andrus and drummer Gus Johnson for Columbia in 1962 with tributes to Barney Bigard, Pee Wee Russell, Jimmy Noone and some of the other greats of the instrument. At the time Woody was using a sextet which included Nat, Chuck, trumpeter Bill Chase, tenorist Gordon Brisker and drummer Jimmy Campbell. Concurrently trombonist Phil Wilson was in the army with the North American Air Defence Command band. Phil remembers being with the NORAD band at the Michigan State Fair.

'Woody was nearby playing a place called The Rooster Tail and Nat and Chase and all of them came out to see us because we were all good friends. Chase, Brisker and Jake Hanna and I had played together in Herb Pomeroy's band in Boston from 1955 to 1957. Chase told me that Nat was working on Woody to reform the band and asked if I was interested. I told him emphatically yes, and that I would be out of the army in a few months and free to join. Nat got Jake from Harry James.

'Nat worked out a deal with Woody that Nat would run the band and Woody would just front it to get it started, Nat knowing that when it was good enough Woody would take control. That's the way it happened. When the band took shape there were twelve of us who'd played in the Pomeroy band. And all of us wanted to make it a classic Herd so bad that we could taste it. We came together in May 1962 and, thanks to the invaluable experience with Herb Pomeroy, we knew the importance of proper rehearsing and we knew *how* to rehearse, which eased the way a lot.'

The Swinging Herd, as it was to be known, *did* become a classic band to place alongside the First and Second Herds. The combination of the Herman tradition, personified in Woody and Nat Pierce, coupled with the technical expertise of the young Bostonians produced a fierce and polished band capable of turning out classics almost at the drop of a hat.

74

There were virtuosi in every department. Bill Chase led the trumpets with enormous stamina and he and the more lyrical Paul Fontaine took the trumpet solos. Phil Wilson, soon to be joined by his disciple Henry Southall, played pyrotechnical trombone with a soul fervour that came largely from Vic Dickenson. An unlikely builder's labourer, who was to return to that trade in later times, articulated his tenor solos with a speed previously unheard of. His name was Sal Nistico and he announced himself to the world with a blistering performance on the band's first recording dates on 15 and 16 October 1962. Nat Pierce was fired with enthusiasm and was turning out some of the best writing of his life. He worked out an irresistible version of Horace Silver's *Sister Sadie* which featured Sal's flashing tenor and swinging, shouting band ensembles as potent as any since the First Herd. Even now, looking back, it is difficult to find a flaw in the band. Jake Hanna was in the Dave Tough-Don Lamond class, bassist Andrus could play faster than anyone Woody had ever had, and Pierce was able to create from the piano any mood that the music required. One of the sensations of that first album was *It's A Lonesome Old Town* which had Wilson stretching the trombone technique to the outer limits. He also shattered glasses with his bursting solo on the eight minute *Camel Walk*, a Bill Chase composition which also featured Woody, Chuck and tenorist Gordon Brisker. The band abounded with good jazz soloists who always played as if they meant it. There was never room in a Herman band for hot air men. Phil Wilson told the author 'By 1962, with the sometime exception of Charlie Mingus's music, jazz musicians had turned inwards and become introverted. Woody's extrovert new band knocked some sense into them. Nat was one of the strong influences. He had a wonderful knowledge of Duke Ellington and Basie and deep roots in the big band tradition.'

Nat became the band manager, or straw boss. 'It's a thankless job. No matter what you do, you're always wrong,' he told the author. 'The band leader most times goes on his merry way and leaves you to worry about the band. You have to get the musicians to leave early in case there's a delay from heavy traffic, and they think it will be alright if they leave later. So there's hassle before you've even moved. Then somebody's wife is sick, and you have to find a substitute player for tonight. The bus broke down. Somebody left his trumpet behind. You've got to call ahead for hotel reservations. It's impossible. And it's all wrong. Comes out wrong each time. How can you juggle with 16 or 17 people and move them over hundreds of miles each day and *not* have things go wrong?'

The band took up residence at the Metropole in New York. Mainly for drinkers, it wasn't well endowed with space for a band, and the Herd stood on a narrow raised platform behind the bar with the brass lined up to Woody's left and the saxes and rhythm to his right. It was hard for the brass to hear the saxophones and vice versa. Nevertheless the music was sensational, and nobody fell off the platform.

In December 1962 the band recorded for SESAC again cutting a dozen arrangements by Nat, Phil, Bill Chase and Gene Roland. Nobody could suppress this great band, and once again the music had a vitality that could only be matched by one of the Basie bands. Oddly enough the band included Basie's Freddie Green on guitar, probably at Nat's instigation, because he and Freddie were friends, and also Duke's tenor man Paul Gonsalves, making an unusual but potent substitute for Sal Nistico.

Moving over to the West Coast, the Herd opened at the Basin Street West in Los Angeles in May 1963 for three nights. Mary Ann McCall and Red Norvo dropped by, and the audience included Sarah Vaughan, Joe Williams, Johnny Mercer and Nat Cole amongst the star visitors. CBS recorded 32 titles from the band's stay, and most of them remain unissued. However eight of them comprised the 'Encore' album that won a Grammy award as the best big band album of the year. The band was booked to play at the Grammy ceremony and had five pieces of music for each category. When the winner in each was announced there was a mad scramble amongst the musicians to find the appropriate chart.

Louis Armstrong had been nominated for an award for his recording of *Hello Dolly*, and he played for two hours with his pianist Billy Kyle and Woody, Phil Wilson, Chuck Andrus and Jake Hanna from the Herd. 'That was the fastest two hours of my musical life', recalled Wilson. 'A joy, an absolute joy!'

Five of the charts on 'Encore' were Nat Pierce's including the original *That's Where It Is*, a feature for Nat's piano with an effective tag from *Silent Night*. Nat's arrangement of *Days Of Wine And Roses* invested the Mancini tune with a new elegance and Henry Southall was allowed his head on *Watermelon Man* and *Jazz Me Blues*, wherein he trod Wilson country. Phil had his turn on *Body And Soul,* one of Nat's earlier efforts, which had lovely alto from the Chopper.

In 1964 several interesting new men came in. The eloquent trumpeter Dusko Goykovich became one of the first of a long line of European players to grace the ranks. The tenors changed completely during the year and by September included Gary Klein, Raoul Romero and the brilliant Andy McGhee, all fine soloists. Ex-Dizzy Gillespie vocalist Joe Carroll was also added.

An unpleasant incident occurred when the band was due to play at a country club in Arizona. When the band went to eat at the club it was refused service because Andy McGhee and Joe Carroll were black. 'We walked out of the club, we weren't going to play,' remembered Wilson. 'The manager came over and asked where we were going, so we explained the situation. "What would it take to keep you here?" he asked. "Well," Woody said, "you can fire whoever that was who refused to serve us, and we get a free sit-down meal for the whole band, then we'll stay and play for you, maybe." And we got it. They fired the guy, but that was tokenism, and they'd have taken him back on afterwards.'

On 9 September the band recorded again live at Harrah's Club in the resort of Lake Tahoe. The solo and writing strength was prodigious with a notable Bill Holman arrangement of Ellington's *Just Squeeze Me,* a couple of potent Pierce charts, and Phil Wilson's *Wa-Wa Blues* with a remarkable duet between Phil and Joe Carroll's vocal imitation of a trombone.

As far as recordings were concerned at this period the wild jazz thrashes were most often recorded live, whilst the studio recordings were more disciplined and straight faced. Holman and Pierce each contributed three good charts to the 'My Kind Of Broadway' collection and trumpeter Don Rader, with Woody in 1959, joined Yugoslavian Goykovich in the section and, like Dusko, wrote a chart for the album.

The band began the regular series of European and later world wide tours which was to continue for the next two decades. The remarkable spirit and the strong solo team impressed audiences everywhere. Well, almost everywhere. On a State Department sponsored tour of Africa the band played a concert before a silent crowd of villagers. Observing the lack of audience reaction Woody pressed on with his normal programme. As the Herd roared to the climax of the

The 1957 Herd at The Blue Note Club, Chicago. Photo Bobby Lamb
Woody leads. Trumpets: Bill Berry, Bill Castagnino, Johnny Coppola, Danny Stiles, Andy Peele. Trombones: Willie Dennis, Bill Harris, Bobby Lamb. Reeds: Bob Newman, Jim Cooke, Jay Migliori, Don Seens. Vibes: Victor Feldman. Bass: John Peel. Drums: Don Michaels. Pianist Vince Guaraldi is obscured.

last number the audience dispersed as silently as it had come.

Woody was enchanted with the first of his many visits to Poland, his grandfather's homeland, and he renewed friendships made in England with the Anglo American Herd in 1959.

As well as the now annual trips abroad, the Herd remained effective at home. Another trip to the Basin Street West in San Francisco during June 1965 resulted in the 'Woody's Winners' set of recordings which was jazz music of the highest standards. The ten minute version of *Opus De Funk* out-roared and out-swung the original Capitol version, and the driving band riffs were heralded by an inspiring and lengthy solo from Pierce which culminated in an affectionate display of stride piano. Dry as ever, Woody called for 'a nice round of applause for Mary Lou Wiliams', little sensing the mine he was planting, for countless reviews of the record noted that Mary Lou had sat in with the band, and there were lengthy arguments in letters columns ('Woody *says* it's Mary Lou: what more evidence could you want?'). Nat and Mary Lou, who found the whole business hilarious, were constantly approached by worried enthusiasts to set the matter straight, but as late as 1984 Mary Lou was still being incorrectly cited as the pianist. Pierce was prominent on another track, Don Rader's steamy *Greasy Sack Blues* here recorded for the first time, but subsequently a staple of the band's library along with the more established classics. Bill Chase showed the power of the trumpet section in his abrasive chart *23 Red* with Chase, Goykovich and Rader climbing over each other with frantic dexterity. Again Nat swung irresistibly on *Woody's Whistle*, with righteous wailing from Dusko and Sal Nistico. (A tolerant man, Woody marked the point when that tolerance was about to break, by blowing a whistle. All the musicians respected this device.)

Saddened by what he regarded as the arid futility of the 'ghost' bands — bands which were kept touring the world after their leaders were long dead, Woody told his family that the Herds would cease to exist when he did. He was determined that there would be no posthumous Woody Herman Band.

While his charm and patience are famous, he is a tough man who expects and gets the best. Only occasionally does irritation show through. On one occasion when he was auditioning a Spanish trumpet player who was not very good but persisted in proving it at great length, it surfaced. 'For God's sake,' he bellowed, 'does anyone know the Spanish for "stop"?'

Chapter Six

From 1963 on the Herman band was more or less continuously in business. There was a constant tide in and out of the band as musicians left, returned and left again. As we have seen the cost of moving such a large group of men about the world was high, and there were also hidden payouts that Herman had to make over the years as a result of confusion over managerial contracts — often he found himself paying two groups of people for the same service. Always an honourable man with the highest reputation, he was sometimes stricken with less than efficient management, and the resultant financial problems tended to emerge after the perpetrator of them had left. The low point of such matters occurred when the police came to see him backstage at the Newport Jazz Festival as the result of his manager's failure to settle a long standing bill with a local bus company.

All these costs added up, and what was left emphasised the historical fact that being a sideman in a big band on the road is not the best paid job. The musicians had to settle their own hotel bills in addition to the expense of running their homes. This led to a high turnover in the ranks, with men constantly quitting when they found jobs at home.

But there were advantages in the shifting personnel. Once more Herman tapped a continuing and remarkable lode of young players, as well as attracting returning veterans like Carl Fontana and Sal Nistico. Trumpeter Bill Byrne joined in late 1965 and has stayed for two decades so far. Youngsters of the finest kind, jazz stars of the future once again proliferated in the ranks — saxophonists Bob

Pierson, Frank Vicari, Al Gibbons, Roger Neumann, Joe Romano were all great tenor soloists and dazzling technicians. Joe Temperley from Scotland had new things to say in his hard driving baritone sax style, part Harry Carney, part Temperley. He was eventually succeeded by the great bebop veteran Cecil Payne. Young Bill Watrous joined the returning Henry Southall and veteran Bob Burgess in the trombones, and the tasteful and inventive pianist Al Dailey joined in 1967. The band starred at that year's Monterey Festival and recorded Bill Holman's prodigious suite *Concerto For Herd*, a masterpiece spoiled by poor recording quality. Woody played soprano on *The Horn Of The Fish*, another Holman composition. He came to the instrument after hearing John Coltrane play it in a club one night. Next day Woody went out and bought one, quickly mastering the awkward beast — although it had been made easier to play since the days when only Sidney Bechet and Johnny Hodges could cope with it.

The Monterey set was recorded for Verve. Woody had left CBS earlier that year and in 1968 signed for the Chess company, for whom he appeared on their Cadet label.

Always ready to explore new ideas, the band followed the rush into electronic rhythm sections and the blending of traditional Herman brass and reed sections with electric piano, bass and guitar dismayed some of the older fans but, in the traditional line of Herman philosophy, brought in the young audience to whom the rock beat was the key to unlock the music.

The band recorded a group of pop songs of the day as their first contribution to Cadet, and the album was issued under the title 'Light My Fire'. The Monterey band had by this time, October 1968, given way to an almost completely new line up. Ex-Blakey Messengers pianist John Hicks teamed with drummer Ed Soph in the rhythm section. Soph was to be another recurrent Hermanite. The trumpets blasted *McArthur Park* and Sal Nistico was wreathed with echo for *Hush*, the Deep Purple number. Woody featured on a delicate outsider, *Impression Of Strayhorn*.

Bill Chase returned to the trumpets in time for the next Cadet album, 'Heavy Exposure' when Donny Hathaway on organ and two extra percussionist were added to the band. Nistico and Chase fought their way through it all and Bob Burgess played some good improvisations over the new style rhythm. But the good charts were weighted down by that very heavy section.

Frank Tiberi and Woody Herman, Nice 1983. Photo Tim Motion

Help was at hand, and three remarkable young musicians once
more appeared to change the direction the band took — trumpeters
Tony Klatka and Bill Stapleton and the brilliant young New
Zealander, Alan Broadbent. Broadbent was a most imaginative and
skilful arranger and although he didn't stay long as the band's
pianist, he contributed a string of fine arrangements to the Herd over
the years. He wrote all but one of the arrangements on an album
called simply 'Woody' and they included a remarkable fourteen
minute reworking of *Blues In The Night* which displayed Alan, Sal
Nistico and Tony Klatka as soloists.

By the time Woody signed for the Fantasy label in 1972, Harold
Danko had charge of the electric piano and Tom Anastas, who had
been with the band on baritone in the sixties, returned. Greg Herbert
and Frank Tiberi were on tenors, and both were to be major soloists
in the ensuing years, with Tiberi taking charge of Woody's instruments (Woody rarely warms up and Frank's job, in addition to
keeping the horns in good repair, included wetting the reeds and
handing the horns to Woody as he walked on stage). The first album
was 'The Raven Speaks' mixing pop music with jazz, and producing
traditional blues shout ups and a reworking of Herbie Hancock's

Watermelon Man which for some reason became entitled *Sandia Chicano*.

The second album for Fantasy, the 1973 'Giant Steps', saw the band firmly back on a jazz path with a set of dazzling arrangements by Stapleton, Broadbent and Klatka. Jim Pugh, a young trombonist in the best Herman tradition, played lead and took poised and supple solos, while Andy Laverne took over the keyboards. Laverne brought a new concept to the electronics, widening the sound colours without compromising the music, and at last the rhythm meshed properly with the horns. He lashed the band along on Chick Corea's *La Fiesta*, which also used Greg Herbert on piccolo along with Tiberi on tenor and Woody's soprano. Pugh played a thoughtful *Meaning Of The Blues* and Broadbent had one of his most inventive compositions recorded in *BeBop And Roses*, an imposing exercise in retrospection. The title track, originally a juggernaut exercise for composer John Coltrane, emerged as a chase for Tiberi and Herbert, finally confirming their abilities as outstanding soloists.

Coltrane was represented again on the 'Thundering Herd' album from 1974 when Klatka arranged the haunting *Naima* and Stapleton did Trane's *Lazy Bird*. Klatka also wrote the fine *Blues For Poland* recorded at this session and featuring in addition to Laverne and the composer, the excellent Czech baritone saxist Jan Konopasek.

Poland continued to attract Woody and he returned there in 1976 with a band crammed with prodigious stars. Pugh, Tiberi and Byrne were still there, with Tiberi now playing bassoon to add to tenor and flute. Alongside him was tenorist Gary Anderson, who wrote some formidable charts for the library. A new source of sidemen suddenly opened up. In 1975 Herman had played a jazz festival in Wichita and had heard a trio composed of students from the North Texas State University. This comprised Lyle Mays on keyboards, Kirby Stewart on bass and drummer Steve Houghton. Woody was most impressed and, since he had decided he needed to change the whole attitude of the rhythm section in the band, he took the trio on en bloc.

'It turned out to be a good thing for the school,' bassist Marc Johnson told the author. 'Whenever any of the guys left Woody's rhythm section, they would recommend someone else from North Texas, so we had an open channel to the rhythm section.'

Marc himself eventually joined Woody. 'It was another gradient in my career, because the level of consistency which was demanded of you was quite remarkable. Later, when I joined the Bill Evans Trio, I found the experience with Woody indispensable. I couldn't have done the gig with Bill if it hadn't been for that. Woody's book is so diverse. There are so many styles and idioms that you're asked to play, and to play well, that it's a real challenge. You had to master swing from the forties and the contemporary rock beat and at the same time bend to fit in with such a large group of musicians.'

Back from Europe, the band returned to Carnegie Hall on 20 November 1976 to celebrate Woody's 40th anniversary as a bandleader. It had taken Woody and his manager Hermie Dressel three months to organise the concert, and a representative selection of the hundreds of ex Herdsmen appeared along with the contemporary band. Nat Pierce sat in for his chart of *Apple Honey*, joined by Flip Phillips, Jim Pugh, Phil Wilson, Pete Candoli and Don Lamond, and backed Flip on *Sweet And Lovely*. The Four Brothers were Jimmy Giuffre, Stan Getz, Al Cohn and Zoot Sims, and Mary Ann McCall was there to recreate *Wrap Your Troubles In Dreams* with Nat. Bill Harris was commemorated as Jim Pugh played *Everywhere* and Phil Wilson *Bijou*. Getz was as elegant as ever with *Early Autumn, Blue Serge* and *Blue Getz Blues* with Ralph Burns on piano for *Autumn*. Cohn, Giuffre and Getz were backed by pianist Jimmy Rowles on *Cousins* and the Candoli brothers shared the Klatka chart of *Brotherhood Of Man*. The young Herd was on good form, and contributed two more recent hits, Broadbent's *Blues In The Night* chart and Gary Anderson's rock-propelled version of Copeland's *Fanfare For The Common Man*, even more inspiring in Woody's version, dare it be said, than in Copeland's original! This was an emotional occasion, as one might imagine, and fortunately it was captured for posterity on record. Woody was so carried away that he even forgot to play *Woodchopper's Ball*.

Four months later, in March 1977, came a dreadful contrast to the anniversary. Woody was driving through Kansas when he fell asleep at the wheel and collided with an oncoming car. His injuries were so serious that there were fears for his life, and it seemed out of the question that he would ever lead the band again. Apart from injuries to his body, one of his legs was horribly mangled. As the anxious weeks went by he showed his resilience and his life was no longer in danger. When the weeks turned to months his determination to pull through had him moving gingerly with the help of a walker, and then, incredibly, in late 1977, he was not only back with the band, but the walker became a familiar sight all over Europe as he led the band on tour.

At the beginning of 1978 the band recorded for Century with a galaxy of guest arrangers including Chick Corea, Vic Feldman, Ralph Burns and regulars Stapleton, Anderson and Broadbent, and at the same time cut an album of ballads featuring Flip Phillips on tenor with an added string section.

By now the Monterey Festival was almost synonymous with Herman's name. The roots of the band had really been on the California coast since Woody made his home there in the forties. Los Angeles was full of off-the-road Herdsmen — Nat Pierce, Bill Berry, Bill Perkins, Shorty Rogers, the Candolis, and in addition there was a pool of brilliant young musicians who worked in the Hollywood studios.

Big bands of a very high standard proliferated in the city, led by Frankie Capp and Nat Pierce, Bill Berry, Roger Neumann, Bill Holman, Bob Florence and many others. But these were static, not touring bands like the Herd.

Up north in Concord, wealthy entrepreneur Carl Jefferson had been developing a fine jazz record label as well as his flourishing automobile business. He had issued albums by the best of the West Coast musicians, restricting himself firstly to small groups. But he was anxious to start a big band catalogue, and was fortunate to find the Frankie Capp-Nat Pierce Juggernaut and the Bill Berry LA Big Band more or less on his doorstep. His issues by these bands were immensely successful, with Juggernaut's first album topping the polls in Europe for many months.

To the Berry and Capp-Pierce bands it must have seemed that they were on their way to international status. But fate had it that Nat's old boss had left Fantasy and didn't have a record company. Jefferson moved in surely to begin a lasting and, in Herman terms, very important association between Woody and Concord. Berry and Capp-Pierce were caught in the backwash and there were no more albums from them as Woody's became the house band. Jefferson was obviously determined to promote his new star properly and the albums the band made added top guest stars, and Woody fronted other groups made up from local stars or former sidemen. With no expense spared in production and the band maintaining its normal high standards the albums could hardly fail.

The first one was done on 15 September 1979 at Monterey. In a remarkable example of hedging his bet, Jefferson recorded Getz, Dizzy Gillespie, Slide Hampton and Woody Shaw with the band with Getz as bewitching as ever in the Broadbent chart *What Are You Doing The Rest Of Your Life?* But the band was not outshone by the guests, and Frank Tiberi had another Coltrane tune, *Countdown*, in an arrangement with Frank and Bob Belden on tenors. Dave Lalama, the band's pianist, also followed in the tradition of pianist-arrangers and featured with Woody and baritone Gary Smulyan on Duke's *I Got It Bad*, which Dave had arranged. Slide Hampton arranged two of Dizzy's compositions, *Woody'n' You* and *Manteca* to feature the composer and guests along with drummer Ed Soph.

While the recording side of things went well, the touring band business was very much in decline as the eighties began and even the perennial Count Basie, by now doyen of the bandleaders, was feeling the pinch. As the 'name' leaders of the sixties and seventies parked their buses, Woody cleverly switched the emphasis of the band's work to schools and from the late seventies on as much as 80 per cent was in teaching clinics at colleges throughout America. Woody had initially been persuaded into this field by Stan Kenton, who so imaginatively developed the idea of a jazz clinic. Woody quickly grew to love this kind of work and found that it was good for both the students and the men in the band. It was also financially rewarding and was vital in keeping the Herd together. At that same 1979 Monterey Festival he led a contingent from the California All-Star High School band. A portfolio of 27 of the Herd's arrangements was produced for use in the clinics.

But still costs rose inexorably. The band had to earn $18,000 a week just to keep its head above water, and although the sidemen were making between $300 and $450 a week, expenses on the road had to come out of that.

Much of the strain was taken off Woody by his expert manager Hermie Dressel, and Bill Byrne took care of the road manager's headaches. Woody paced himself sensibly and tried to keep the overnight hops to under 400 miles. He still had pain from his accident, although he claimed to have got used to the clank of the steel rod supporting the various fractures in his leg.

With some fanfare the Herman band took over a club in New Orleans in which Woody had an interest. The idea was for the band to be permanently resident there, and indeed the Chopper was justly honoured by being made King Of The Zulus at the Mardi Gras celebrations. But the venture began as the world recession deepened, and the idea was not a success.

Back on the West Coast, Jefferson pressed ahead with his ideas for Woody, and shifted his outdoor recordings to his own Concord Festival. In 1981 he brought him back to head a group which included two former Herman stars, Jake Hanna and Dave McKenna along with Dick Johnson, Cal Tjader and youngsters Scott Hamilton, Cal Collins, Warren Vache and Bob Maize. Oddly enough the presence of Japanese clarinettist Eiji Kitamura on this session emphasised the heat and potency of Herman's playing and showed once again what a fine jazz soloist he was and is. In July of that year Woody flew to New York for a session with half a dozen old timers from the Herd. This was a four tenor front line with Al Cohn, Sal Nistico, Bill Perkins, Flip Phillips, John Bunch, George Duvivier and Don Lamond. The music was vigorous and energetic with a tasteful selection of early hits including *Tiny's Blues, Four Others, Not Really the Blues* and *The Goof And I,* along with a fine new Cohn composition, *Woody's Lament.* In such bustling company Woody restricted himself to playing alto on *Tenderly.* It was notable, as was confirmed in succeeding years, that Flip Phillips's playing was getting better and better.

Stan Getz and Al Cohn returned to guest with the band at the 1982 Concord Festival, and by now there was another new and splendid pianist/arranger, John Oddo, who wrote four of the compositions on the subsequent Concord album and arranged most of the others. Bill Holman contributed *Midnight Run,* which featured Woody, Bill Stapleton on fluegelhorn and a new ebullient character on trumpet, George Rabbai. Bill also wrote the band arrangement of *The Dolphin* to showcase Getz. *Lemon Drop* reappeared after many years with Rabbai singing the bop vocal and Cohn particularly on form. New names and good soloists abounded as usual — John Fedchock on trombone, Randy Russell and Bill Ross on tenors and Oddo himself at the piano. The album received a Grammy nomination.

In September 1982 the band toured Japan. Stapleton was replaced by Bill Byrne who had missed the Concord Festival, as indeed had Frank Tiberi who now came back to replace Russell. The band had always been so popular in Japan that its presence on its own was enough to fill the various halls, but Al Cohn, Med Flory, Sal Nistico and Flip Phillips had been added to the tour as guests, and the success was overwhelming. The Concord album which resulted showed the usual exotic mixture of titles, with standards like *Four Brothers* and Rader's *Greasy Sack Blues* alongside Chick Corea's *Crystal Silence*, Flip's *The Claw* (for the tenors) and Oddo's chart of *Rockin' Chair* with a good humoured vocal duet between George Rabbai and Woody and space for Rabbai to tread Armstrong ground with his trumpet solo.

Back in the States the band recorded for Concord with Rosemary Clooney, another of the label's big successes. John Oddo wrote all of the arrangements save one, and the session offered a fine chance to hear the quality of the section work. It seems likely that Oddo is to tread the paths made by Ralph Burns and Nat Pierce, because his writing for the band has great substance and depth. Miss Clooney is fortunate in having such support, as an ear bent to the arrangement of *Summer Knows* will demonstrate.

The big band was working mainly out West as 1984 drew to a close, and Woody began 1985 by taking a small group of alumni into New York's St Regis Hotel. Among the names he planned to use were Carl Fontana, John Bunch, Al Cohn, Flip Phillips and Jake Hanna.

Then disaster struck. It had been discovered that there were huge tax irregularities in the band's affairs of the middle sixties, at a time when the manager Abe Turchen looked after the money. It transpired that Turchen had set money aside for payment to the Internal Revenue Service (including the tax due from the individual musicians) and instead of paying it over had gambled it all away. By the time all this came to light Turchen had died and Woody was held responsible for the full amount and was in grave danger of being sent to jail. The I.R.S. has been relentless in pursuing the old man for the full amount and he has to keep working to pay them or risk having all his possessions seized (there is currently a rumour that the Service is trying to seize the Hollywood home that Woody and Charlotte bought from Humphrey Bogart and Lauren Bacall back in the forties).

It is a sad commentary on the American way of doing things that an honourable man should be hounded and have his last years over-shadowed by reprisals for something that was not of his doing. Surely there must be someone in authority who could write the matter off and leave Woody to enjoy a peaceful old age.

Although he was obviously suffering from severe exhaustion

Phil Wilson, '... if only...' Photo Tim Motion

Woody toured Europe in the summer of 1985 with a magnificent group of all stars: Harry Edison on trumpet, Buddy Tate and Al Cohn on tenors, John Bunch on piano, bassist Steve Wallace and drummer Jake Hanna. The music was magnificent with Cohn and Tate particularly striking sparks from each other. Woody, not a hundred per cent fit, had lost some of his fluency on clarinet, but he showed on *I've Got The World On A String* his vocal abilities were little impaired—the breakneck *Caldonia* would have thrown a Jon Hendricks, never mind Woody! The musicians in the band showed great concern for the leader and Buddy Tate in particular took care of Woody and his affairs.

Woody had a big band ready for the beginning of 1986, the year of his 50th anniversary as a bandleader. The new library drew heavily on Ellington material and the new Herd was every bit as skilled and effective as the earlier ones. It was notable that the old man's clarinet playing had recovered from the frailty that had been noticeable in his work at the 1985 Nice Jazz Festival. Although it was not to go away and would remain with him for life, he seemed to be philosophical about the burden of his tax problems.

Woody Herman and his Herds have conquered the hemispheres, and his bands are as popular throughout Asia as they are in Europe, as much in demand to work in Los Angeles as in New York. Herman goes on and claims, as he says in the letter to the author printed elsewhere in this book, that he is too old to retire. There is an old adage that if you always want to look young, you should hang around with very old people. Herman has achieved that end by reversing the formula. He always works with young people. One of the greatest achievements of any Herd is the potent dispensation of energy. Energy comes best from young people, but with the experience of the old coach to guide them, it is always deployed to maximum effect.

Of course, you must have the right young people, and one of Herman's talents is in spotting potential greatness in a player before anyone else does (Charlie Parker had this ability as instanced by the way in which he selected the apparently musically incoherent Miles Davis for his group — Parker knew then about Miles what we all know now). Another important quality is Woody's unerring ability to edit a performance on the stand. He knows exactly when to cut a soloist off or, if the man is in full flight and likely to add something constructive, when to let him take an extra couple of choruses without destroying the balance of the arrangement. He looks forward, hates to look back, and if you ask him which was the best band he ever had he'll answer 'The next one'.

On the face of it the formula is fairly simple. Take a team of good soloists, add some good section leaders, a rhythm section with roots, some good writers and a player-coach. Anyone could do it.

Or could they? Phil Wilson's thought is a wise one.

'Nobody does what Woody does as well as he does. If we could only figure out what it is he does . . .'

Bibliography

This book could not have been written without reference to the following sources:

Feather, Leonard: *The Encyclopedia Of Jazz, The Encyclopedia Of Jazz In The Sixties*, and *The Encyclopedia Of Jazz In The Seventies*. New York, Bonanza Books, London, Quartet.

George Hall: liner notes to Hindsight HSR-116 and HSR-134, Hindsight Records Inc., P.O. Box 7114-R, Burbank, CA. 91510.

Albert McCarthy: *Big Band Jazz*, Barrie & Jenkins Ltd., London.

George T. Simon: *The Big Bands*, The Macmillan Company, New York.

Igor Stravinsky and Robert Craft: *Conversations With Stravinsky*, Faber Music Ltd., London.

James A. Treichel: *Woody Herman And The Second Herd*, Joyce Music Publication, Box 1707, Zephyrhills, FLA 33599.

Eric Walter White: *Stravinsky*, Faber & Faber, London & Boston.

Special thanks are due to Eddie Cook, publisher of *Jazz Journal International*, for permission to quote from the author's contributions to that magazine and to make use of its library of photographs.

Selected Discography

As Woody Herman's recording career began in the early thirties, a complete discography would be far too long for a book of this size. Fortunately almost all of Woody's more significant work has appeared on LP, although unfortunately at the time of writing some of these LPs are only obtainable from specialist second-hand dealers. Original American and British catalogue numbers are given (those for stereophonic issues, where they differ from mono numbers, are given in brackets). With a major artist of Woody Herman's stature, many of these LPs are likely to be reissued at any time and readers are advised to consult their dealers regarding current availability and catalogue numbers.

Material recorded since December 1948 is listed in an album-by-album format, as reissues from this period almost always duplicate earlier LPs, usually retaining the original album title. Titles recorded before December 1948 have been given reference numbers to identify their LP releases; a key to these numbers is at the end of the listing.

The listing has been prepared from a variety of sources, but I am particularly grateful for Brian Rust's *Jazz Records 1897 — 1942* and Jorgen Grunnet Jepsen's *Jazz Records 1942 — 1962*. A feature in the October 1983 issue of the IAJRC Journal ('Touching Up Jepsen', collated by Bruce D. Davidson) was also most helpful, as it included many corrections to session dates for items recorded for Capitol and Columbia. Thanks are due to Brian Davis and Steve Voce for answering specific queries, and particularly to Alun Morgan, who gave me complete access to his record collection and filing system when I was checking my draft.

Since the beginning of 1941, Woody Herman has used a few bars of his theme tune *Blue Flame* to open and close his public appearances, but in the majority of cases I have omitted this title when listing recordings of broadcasts.

The country of release of each LP has been given using the following abbreviations:–

(A)	United States of America	(F)	France
(E)	United Kingdom	(H)	Holland

Instrumental abbreviations are as follows:–

(as)	alto saxophone	(g)	guitar
(b)	string bass	(p)	piano
(bs)	baritone saxophone	(pc)	percussion
(btp)	bass trumpet	(ss)	soprano saxophone
(cga)	conga drums	(tb)	trombone
(cl)	clarinet	(tp)	trumpet
(cls)	celeste	(ts)	tenor saxophone
(d)	drums	(v)	vocal
(eb)	electric bass	(vb)	vibraphone
(ep)	electronic piano	(vn)	violin
(f)	flute	(ww)	woodwinds
(flh)	fluegel horn		

TONY SHOPPEE
November 1985

WOODY HERMAN AND HIS ORCHESTRA

Clarence Willard, Kermit Simmons (tp), Joe Bishop (flh), Neil Reid (tb), Woody Herman (cl, as, v), Murray Williams, Don Watt (as), Saxie Mansfield, Bruce Wilkins (ts), Horace Diaz (p), Chick Reeves (g), Walter Yoder (b), Frank Carlson (d). *New York, April 26, 1937*
DUPREE BLUES vWH   (1)/TROUBLE IN MIND

Clarence Willard, Kermit Simmons (tp), Joe Bishop (flh), Neil Reid (tb), Woody Herman (cl, as, v), Jack Ferrier (as), Deane Kincaide (as, tb), Saxie Mansfield, Bruce Wilkins (ts), Nick Hupfer (vn), Tommy Linehan (p), Oliver Mathewson (g), Walter Yoder (b), Frank Carlson (d).

New York, September 23, 1937

EXACTLY LIKE YOU/REMEMBER ME/CAN'T WE BE FRIENDS?/MUSKRAT RAMBLE/JAZZ
ME BLUES/OLD MAN MOON/AIN'T MISBEHAVIN'/SOMEDAY SWEETHEART/SQUEEZE
ME/WEARY BLUES   (2)

Ray Hopfner (as), Pete Johns (ts) replace Deane Kincaide and Bruce Wilkins.
New York, November 1937
YOU TOOK THE WORDS RIGHT OUT OF MY HEART vWH/I CAN'T BE BOTHERED NOW/
ROYAL GARDEN BLUES/APACHE DANCE/BOB WHITE vWH/QUEEN ISABELLA   (2)

WOODY HERMAN AND HIS WOODCHOPPERS
Joe Bishop (flh), Woody Herman (cl, v), Tommy Linehan (p), Hy White (g), Walter
Yoder (b), Frank Carlson (d).   *New York, December 22, 1938*
RIVER BED BLUES vWH   (1)

WOODY HERMAN AND HIS ORCHESTRA
Clarence Willard, Jerry Neary (tp), Joe Bishop (flh), Neil Reid (tb), Woody Herman
(cl, as, v), Joe Estren, Ray Hopfner (as), Saxie Mansfield, Pete Johns (ts), Tommy
Linehan (p), Hy White (g), Walter Yoder (b), Frank Carlson (d).   same session
INDIAN BOOGIE WOOGIE   (3)

Mac MacQuordale and Steady Nelson (tp) replace Jerry Neary.
New York, April 12, 1939
AT THE WOODCHOPPER'S BALL   (3, 4)/DALLAS BLUES   (1, 4)/BLUES UPSTAIRS vWH
(1, 4)/BLUES DOWNSTAIRS   (1, 4)

Bob Price (tp) and Joe Denton (as) replace Mac MacQuordale and Joe Estren.
New York, May 24, 1939
CASBAH BLUES   (1, 4)/FAREWELL BLUES   (1)

Bob Price (tp), Steady Nelson (tp, v), Cappy Lewis (cornet), Joe Bishop (flh), Toby
Tyler, Neil Reid (tb), Woody Herman (cl, as, v), Herb Tomkins, Ray Hopfner (as),
Nick Caiazza, Saxie Mansfield (ts), Tommy Linehan (p), Hy White (g), Walter
Yoder (b), Frank Carlson (d).
New York, February 5, 1940
PEACH TREE STREET vWH   (1)/BLUE PRELUDE   (1, 4)

Sammy Armato (ts) replaces Nick Caiazza.   *New York, April 10, 1940*
BESSIE'S BLUES vWH & SN   (1)/HERMAN AT THE SHERMAN   (4)

WOODY HERMAN AND HIS FOUR CHIPS
Woody Herman (cl, v), Tommy Linehan (p), Hy White (g), Walter Yoder (b),
Frank Carlson (d).   *New York, September 9, 1940*
CHIPS' BOOGIE WOOGIE   (3)/CHIPS' BLUES vWH   (1)

WOODY HERMAN AND HIS ORCHESTRA
Bob Price, Steady Nelson, Cappy Lewis (tp), Bud Smith, Jesse Ralph, Neil Reid
(tb), Woody Herman (cl, as), Herb Tomkins, Bill Vitale (as), Mickey Folus, Saxie

94

Mansfield (ts), Tommy Linehan (p), Hy White (g), Walter Yoder (b), Frank Carlson (d). *New York, November 9, 1940*
THE GOLDEN WEDDING   (3, 4)

Johnny Owens (tp), Vic Hamann (tb) and Eddie Scalzi (as) replace Bob Price, Jesse Ralph and Bill Vitale. *New York, February 13, 1941*
BLUE FLAME   (1, 3, 4)/FUR TRAPPER'S BALL   (4)

Ray Linn, Steady Nelson, Cappy Lewis (tp), Jerry Rosa, Vic Hamann, Neil Reid (tb), Woody Herman (cl, as, v), Sam Rubinwitch, Jimmy Horvath (as), Herbie Haymer, Saxie Mansfield (ts), Tommy Linehan (p), Hy White (g), Walter Yoder (b), Frank Carlson (d), Carolyn Grey (v).
Los Angeles, August 21, 1941
BISHOP'S BLUES   (1, 4)/WOODSHEDDIN' WITH WOODY   (3, 4)

Los Angeles, September 10, 1941
BLUES IN THE NIGHT   (4)/THIS TIME THE DREAM'S ON ME

WOODY HERMAN AND HIS FOUR CHIPS
Woody Herman (cl) with same p; g; b; d. same session
YARDBIRD SHUFFLE   (3)

WOODY HERMAN AND HIS ORCHESTRA
Ray Linn, George Seaberg, Cappy Lewis, Billie Rogers (tp); remainder of orchestra as for August 21. *Chicago, November 13, 1941*
LAS CHIAPANECAS   (3)/'TIS AUTUMN vWH & CG   (4)

Joe Howard (tb) and Dave Tough (d) replace Vic Hamann and Frank Carlson.
New York, January 28, 1942
A STRING OF PEARLS   (4)

Chuck Peterson, George Seaberg, Cappy Lewis, Billie Rogers (tp), Wally Nims, Tommy Farr, Neil Reid (tb), Woody Herman (cl, as, v), Sam Rubinwitch, Ed Costanza (as), Mickey Folus, Pete Mondello (ts), Tommy Linehan (p), Hy White (g), Walter Yoder (b), Frank Carlson (d).
Los Angeles, July 24, 1942
FOUR OR FIVE TIMES vWH/DOWN UNDER   (3)

Chuck Peterson, Cappy Lewis and another (tp), Billie Rogers (tp, v), Rod Ogle, Jim Burtch, Neil Reid (tb), Woody Herman (cl, as, v), Les Robinson and another (as), Pete Mondello, Vido Musso (ts), Skippy DeSair (bs), Jimmy Rowles (p), Hy White (g), Walter Yoder (b), Frank Carlson (d).
Los Angeles, spring 1943
AT THE WOODCHOPPER'S BALL   (5)

Similar personnel. *Los Angeles, spring or summer 1943*
DOWN UNDER/BISHOP'S BLUES/TAKING A CHANCE ON LOVE vBR/SALT LAKE CITY
BLUES vBR/WHO DAT UP DERE? vWH/DON'T CRY vBR/FOUR OR FIVE TIMES vWH/THE
G.C.G. JUMP + THEME   (5)

Bobby Guyer, Bill Horan, Billy May (tp), Billie Rogers (tp, v), Joe Quartell, Jim
Burtch, Neil Reid (tb), Woody Herman (cl, as), Les Robinson, Chuck DiMaggio
(as), Pete Mondello, Vido Musso (ts), Skippy DeSair (bs), Jimmy Rowles (p), Hy
White (g), Gene Sargent (b), Frank Carlson (d).
Los Angeles, summer 1943
SPRUCE JUICE/I DON'T BELIEVE IN RUMOURS vBR   (5)

Personnel similar to next, featuring Woody Herman (cl) and Johnny Bothwell
(as). *late 1943*
STARLIGHT SOUVENIERS   (5)

Ray Wetzel, Bobby Guyer, Benny Stabler, Nick Travis, Cappy Lewis (tp), Al
Mastren, Ed Kiefer, Eddie Bert (tb), Woody Herman (cl, as, v), Johnny Bothwell,
Chuck DiMaggio (as), Pete Mondello, Ben Webster (ts), Skippy DeSair (bs), Dick
Kane (p), Hy White (g), Chubby Jackson (b), Cliff Leeman (d).
New York, November 18, 1943
DO NOTHING TILL YOU HEAR FROM ME vWH/(b)BASIE'S BASEMENT   (6)/WHO DAT UP
DERE? vWH   (3, 4)

Omit Benny Stabler (tp); Allen Eager (ts) added; Ralph Burns (p) replaces Dick
Kane. *New York, January 8, 1944*
NOAH vWH/I'VE GOT YOU UNDER MY SKIN/I GET A KICK OUT OF YOU/I'LL GET BY
vWH/CRYING SANDS   (6)

Ray Wetzel, Bobby Guyer, Mario Serritello, Neal Hefti (tp), Ed Kiefer, Ed Bennett,
Al Esposito (tb), Woody Herman (cl, as, v), Ernie Caceres, Chuck DiMaggio (as),
Pete Mondello, Budd Johnson (ts), Skippy DeSair (bs), Ralph Burns (p), Hy White
(g), Chubby Jackson (b), Cliff Leeman (d), Frances Wayne (v).
New York, March 23, 1944
CHERRY   (6)/MILKMAN KEEP THOSE BOTTLES QUIET vWH   (6)/IRRESISTABLE YOU
vFW   (3)/IT MUST BE JELLY ('CAUSE JAM DON'T SHAKE LIKE THAT) vWH & FW   (6)

Nick Travis (tp) and Georgie Auld (ts) replace Neal Hefti and Budd Johnson.
New York, March 29, 1944
INGIE SPEAKS   (6)

Ray Wetzel, Billy Robbins, Mario Serritello, Ray Nance, Neal Hefti (tp), Ed Kiefer,
Al Esposito, Juan Tizol (tb), Woody Herman (cl), Chuck DiMaggio, Johnny
Hodges (as), Pete Mondello, Herbie Fields (ts), Skippy DeSair (bs), Ralph Burns
(p), Billy Bauer (g), Chubby Jackson (b), Red Saunders (d).
New York, April 5, 1944
PERDIDO   (6)

Ray Wetzel, Dick Munson, Conte Candoli, Pete Candoli, Neal Hefti (tp), Ed Kiefer, Ralph Pfeffner, Bill Harris (tb), Woody Herman (cl, as, v), Sam Marowitz, Bill Shine (as), Pete Mondello, Flip Phillips (ts), Skippy DeSair (bs), Ralph Burns (p), Billy Bauer (g), Chubby Jackson (b), Dave Tough (d), Frances Wayne (v).

New York, August 2, 1944

IT MUST BE JELLY ('CAUSE JAM DON'T SHAKE LIKE THAT) vWH & FW.   (7)

New York, August 16, 1944

G.I. JIVE vWH   (7)

New York, August 23, 1944

RED TOP/BLUES ON PARADE   (7)

New York, August 30, 1944

JONES BEACHHEAD/FOUR OR FIVE TIMES vWH   (7)

Carl Warwick, Chuck Frankhauser (tp) and John La Porta (as) replace Dick Munson, Conte Candoli and Bill Shine.

New York, September 13, 1944

125TH STREET PROPHET/SOMEBODY LOVES ME vWH   (7)

New York, September 20, 1944

BASIE'S BASEMENT/THERE'LL BE A HOT TIME IN THE TOWN OF BERLIN vWH   (7)

New York, late August/September, 1944

SWEET LORRAINE vWH   (7)

New York, September 27, 1944

IS YOU IS OR IS YOU AIN'T MY BABY vWH   (7)

WOODY HERMAN AND THE WOODCHOPPERS
Neal Hefti (tp), Bill Harris (tb), Woody Herman (cl), Flip Phillips (ts), Marjorie Hyams (vb), Ralph Burns (p), Billy Bauer (g), Chubby Jackson (b), Dave Tough (d).   *New York, September 27, 1944*

1-2-3-4 JUMP   (7, 8)

WOODY HERMAN AND HIS ORCHESTRA
Personnel as for September 20.   *New York, October 4, 1944*

APPLE HONEY   (7)

WOODY HERMAN AND THE WOODCHOPPERS
As previous Woodchoppers personnel of September 27.

Hollywood Palladium, Los Angeles, November 21, 1944

SKYSCRAPER   (8)

WOODY HERMAN AND HIS ORCHESTRA
Personnel as for September 20, plus Marjorie Hyams (vb).

Los Angeles, December 11 & 12, 1944

AS LONG AS I LIVE vFW/I AIN'T GOT NOTHIN' BUT THE BLUES vWH   (6)

WOODY HERMAN AND THE WOODCHOPPERS.
Charlie Shavers (tp), Bill Harris (tb), Woody Herman (cl), Herbie Fields (as), Flip
Phillips, Don Byas, Georgie Auld (ts), Marjorie Hyams (vb), Ralph Burns (p), Billy
Bauer (g), Chubby Jackson (b), Johnny Blowers (d).

Vanderbilt Theatre, New York, January 24, 1945

NORTHWEST PASSAGE (labelled J.P. VANDERBILT IV)   (8)

WOODY HERMAN AND HIS ORCHESTRA
Ray Wetzel, Carl Warwick, Chuck Frankhauser, Pete Candoli, Sonny Berman (tp),
Ed Kiefer, Ralph Pfeffner, Bill Harris (tb), Woody Herman (cl, as, v), Sam Marowitz,
John La Porta (as), Pete Mondello, Flip Phillips (ts), Skippy DeSair (bs), Marjorie
Hyams (vb), Ralph Burns (p), Billy Bauer (g), Chubby Jackson (b), Dave Tough
(d), Frances Wayne (v).

The Meadowbrook, Cedar Grove, New Jersey, February 18, 1945

RED TOP/SATURDAY NIGHT IS THE LONELIEST NIGHT OF THE WEEK vFW/CHUBBY'S
BLUES vWH/HAPPINESS IS JUST A THING CALLED JOE vFW/I DIDN'T KNOW ABOUT
YOU vWH/NORTHWEST PASSAGE   (9)

New York, February 19, 1945

LAURA vWH/APPLE HONEY/I WONDER vWH   (11)

New York, February 26, 1945

CALDONIA vWH/HAPPINESS IS JUST A THING CALLED JOE vFW   (11)

New York, March 1, 1945

GOOSEY GANDER/NORTHWEST PASSAGE/A KISS GOODNIGHT vWH/I'VE GOT THE
WORLD ON A STRING vWH   (11)

Bobby Guyer (tp) replaces Ray Wetzel.

Hotel Sherman, Chicago, March 22, 1945

GOOSEY GANDER/HAPPINESS IS JUST A THING CALLED JOE vFW/I WONDER vWH/
APPLE HONEY   (10)

Ray Linn, Neal Hefti, Conte Candoli, Pete Candoli, Sonny Berman (tp), Ed Kiefer,
Ralph Pfeffner, Bill Harris (tb), Woody Herman (cl, as, v), Sam Marowitz, John La
Porta (as), Pete Mondello, Flip Phillips (ts), Skippy DeSair (bs), Tony Aless (p),
Billy Bauer (g), Chubby Jackson (b), Dave Tough (d), Frances Wayne (v).

Hotel Pennsylvania, New York, July 23, 1945

KATUSHYA vWH/AND THERE YOU ARE vFW/BIJOU/JUNE COMES AROUND EVERY
YEAR vWH/GOOSEY GANDER/I DON'T CARE WHO KNOWS IT vFW/A KISS GOODNIGHT
vWH/APPLE HONEY   (9)

DON'T WORRY 'BOUT THE MULE vWH/I DON'T CARE WHO KNOWS IT vFW/GOOD, GOOD, GOOD vWH/GOOSEY GANDER/THERE'S NO YOU vFW/I NEVER THOUGHT I'D SING THE BLUES vWH/NORTHWEST PASSAGE   (10)

New York, August 20, 1945
THE GOOD EARTH/PUT THAT RING ON MY FINGER vWH/BIJOU   (11)

Irv Lewis (tp) and Red Norvo (vb) added; Buddy Rich (d) replaces Dave Tough.
New York, September 5, 1945
GEE BUT IT'S GOOD TO HOLD YOU vFW/YOUR FATHER'S MOUSTACHE vWH(11)

Personnel as for July 23, except that Irv Lewis (tp) replaces Ray Linn.
New York, September 8, 1945
WILD ROOT   (11)

Irv Lewis, Neal Hefti, Shorty Rogers, Pete Candoli, Sonny Berman (tp), Ed Kiefer, Ralph Pfeffner, Bill Harris (tb), Woody Herman (cl, as v), Sam Marowitz, John La Porta (as), Mickey Folus, Flip Phillips (ts), Sam Rubinwitch (bs), Tony Aless (p), Billy Bauer (g), Chubby Jackson (b), Don Lamond (d), Frances Wayne (v).
New York, December 10, 1945
BLOWIN' UP A STORM   (11 – edited)/LET IT SNOW vWH   (12)

Red Norvo (vb) added; Arnold Fishkin (b) replaces Chubby Jackson.
New York, January 3, 1946
WELCOME TO MY DREAM vFW   (12)

WOODY HERMAN AND THE WOODCHOPPERS
Sonny Berman (tp), Bill Harris (tb), Woody Herman (cl), Flip Phillips (ts), Red Norvo (vb), Tony Aless (p), Billy Bauer (g), Chubby Jackson (b), Don Lamond (d).   *New York, January 1946*
I GOT RHYTHM   (8)

New York, February 8, 1946
BACK TALK/SERGEANT ON A FURLOUGH   (8)

WOODY HERMAN AND HIS ORCHESTRA
Conrad Gozzo, Irvin Markowitz, Shorty Rogers, Pete Candoli, Sonny Berman (tp), Ed Kiefer, Ralph Pfeffner, Bill Harris (tb), Woody Herman (cl, as, v), Sam Marowitz, John La Porta (as), Mickey Folus, Flip Phillips (ts), Sam Rubinwitch (bs), Red Norvo (vb), Tony Aless (p), Billy Bauer (g), Chubby Jackson (b), Don Lamond (d).   *New York, February 17, 1946*
PANACEA vWH   (12)

WOODY HERMAN AND THE WOODCHOPPERS
As previous Woodchoppers personnel of February 8.
Michigan Theatre, Detroit, February 22, 1946
GUNG HO   (8)

Toronto, March 1, 1946

GLOMMED   (8)

Indianapolis, March 15, 1946

FLIP THE WHIP   (8)

WOODY HERMAN AND HIS ORCHESTRA
Previous full personnel as for February 17.

Carnegie Hall, New York, March 25, 1946

BIJOU/SWEET AND LOVELY/SUPERMAN WITH A HORN/BLOWIN' UP A STORM/THE MAN I LOVE/FOUR MEN ON A HORSE/THE GOOD EARTH/YOUR FATHER'S MOUSTACHE/ EVERYWHERE/MEAN TO ME/RED TOP/PANACEA vWH/HALLELUJAH/HEADS UP –1/WILD ROOT   (14)
– 1: This title by the Woodchoppers (personnel as for February 8)

WOODY HERMAN AND THE WOODCHOPPERS
Sonny Berman (tp), Bill Harris (tb), Woody Herman (cl, v), Flip Phillips (ts), Red Norvo (vb), Jimmy Rowles (p), Billy Bauer (g), Chubby Jackson (b), Don Lamond (d).   *Lincoln Auditorium, Syracuse, April 12, 1946*
HEADS UP   (8)

Minneapolis, April 19, 1946

PAPALOMA   (8)

Shorty Rogers (tp) added.   *Chicago, May 13, 1946*
IGOR   (12)

Chicago, May 16, 1946

STEPS/FAN IT vWH   (12)

Chicago, May 20, 1946

NERO'S CONCEPTION/LOST WEEKEND/PAM   (12)

Shorty Rogers omitted.   *Chicago, May 24, 1946*
FAN IT vWH   (8)

Eastwood Gardens, Detroit, June 7, 1946

IGOR   (8)

WOODY HERMAN AND HIS ORCHESTRA
Conrad Gozzo, Cappy Lewis, Shorty Rogers, Pete Candoli, Sonny Berman (tp), Ed Kiefer, Ralph Pfeffner, Neil Reid, Bill Harris (tb), Woody Herman (cl, as), Sam Marowitz, John La Porta (as), Mickey Folus, Flip Phillips (ts), Sam Rubinwitch (bs), Red Norvo (vb), Jimmy Rowles (p), Chuck Wayne (g), Joe Mondragon (b), Don Lamond (d), Mary Ann McCall (v).

Los Angeles, September 17, 1946

THE SIDEWALKS OF CUBA   (12)

100

LADY MCGOWAN'S DREAM (Parts 1 & 2) –1/ROMANCE IN THE DARK vMAM   (12)

SUMMER SEQUENCE (Parts 1 to 3) –1   (13)
– 1: Ralph Burns (p) replaces Jimmy Rowles

EVERYWHERE/WITH SOMEONE NEW/WRAP YOUR TROUBLES IN DREAMS vMAM/BACK TALK   (13)

WOODY HERMAN AND THE WOODCHOPPERS

Sonny Berman (tp), Bill Harris (tb) Woody Herman (cl), Flip Phillips (ts), Red Norvo (vb), Jimmy Rowles (p), Chuck Wayne (g), Joe Mondragon (b), Don Lamond (d).   *Los Angeles, October 12, 1946*
I SURRENDER DEAR/SOMEDAY SWEETHEART   (12)

WOODY HERMAN AND HIS ORCHESTRA

Conrad Gozzo, Chuck Peterson, Cappy Lewis, Al Porcino, Bob Peck (tp), Ed Kiefer, Ralph Pfeffner, Bill Harris (tb), Woody Herman (cl), Sam Marowitz, John La Porta (as), Flip Phillips (ts), Sam Rubinwitch (bs), Jimmy Rowles (p), Chuck Wayne (g), Joe Mondragon (b), Don Lamond (d).   *Chicago, December 10, 1946*
AT THE WOODCHOPPER'S BALL   (12)

NON-ALCOHOLIC   (13)

Bernie Glow, Stan Fishelson, Irvin Markowitz, Shorty Rogers, Ernie Royal (tp), Ollie Wilson, Earl Swope, Bob Swift (tb), Woody Herman (cl, as, v), Sam Marowitz (as), Herbie Steward (ts, as), Stan Getz, Zoot Sims (ts), Serge Chaloff (bs), Fred Otis (p), Gene Sargent (g), Walter Yoder (b), Don Lamond (d), Mary Ann McCall (v).   *Los Angeles, December 19, 1947*
I TOLD YA I LOVE YA, NOW GET OUT vWH   (13)

I'VE GOT NEWS FOR YOU vWH/KEEN AND PEACHY   (13)

THE GOOF AND I/LAZY LULLABY/FOUR BROTHERS/SUMMER SEQUENCE (Part 4) - 1   (13)
- 1: Ralph Burns (p) replaces Fred Otis on this title

P.S. I LOVE YOU vMAM   (13)

Al Cohn (ts) and Jimmy Raney (g) replace Herbie Steward and Gene Sargent.
THE GOOF AND I/THERE'LL BE SOME CHANGES MADE vMAM/BABY I NEED YOU vWH & MAM/THE GOOD EARTH/SWING LOW SWEET CLARINET vMAM/I TOLD YA I LOVE YA,

NOW GET OUT vWH/APPLE HONEY -(edited)   (15)

same location, February 14, 1948

HAPPINESS IS JUST A THING CALLED JOE vMAM   (16)

same location, March 5, 1948

HALF PAST JUMPING TIME/I GOT IT BAD vMAM   (15)

same location, March 6, 1948

LULLABY IN RHYTHM/YOU TURNED THE TABLES ON ME vMAM   (16)

same location, March 7, 1948

MY PAL GONZALES vWH/STARDUST   (15)

same location and period

WILD ROOT   (16)

Harry Babasin (b) replaces Walter Yoder.

Hotel Commodore, New York, April 28, 1948

TINY'S BLUES/WHEN YOU'RE SMILING vMAM/THIS IS NEW/DANCE, BALLERINA, DANCE vMAM   (16)

same location and period

ELEVATION   (16)

same location, May 12, 1948

THE HAPPY SONG/DREAM PEDDLER vMAM/FOUR BROTHERS/I'VE GOT NEWS FOR YOU vWH/KEEN AND PEACHY   (16)

Bill Harris (tb) added; Ralph Burns (p) and Chubby Jackson (b) replace Fred Otis and Harry Babasin.   *Steel Pier, Atlantic City, August 8, 1948*
BERLED IN ERL/NORTHWEST PASSAGE   (15)

Ernie Royal (tp), Stan Getz (ts), Serge Chaloff (bs), Ralph Burns (p), Jimmy Raney (g), Chubby Jackson (b), Don Lamond (d), Woody Herman (v).

same location and date

FAN IT vWH   (15)

Bernie Glow, Stan Fishelson, Irvin Markowitz, Shorty Rogers, Ernie Royal (tp), Ollie Wilson, Earl Swope, Bill Harris, Bob Swift (tb), Woody Herman (cl, as, v), Sam Marowitz (as), Al Cohn, Stan Getz, Zoot Sims (ts), Serge Chaloff (bs), Terry Gibbs (vb), Lou Levy (p), Chubby Jackson (b), Don Lamond (d), Mary Ann McCall (v).   *Royal Roost, New York, October 30,1948*
KEEPER OF THE FLAME/HAPPINESS IS JUST A THING CALLED JOE vMAM/YUCCA/I CAN'T GET STARTED/I'VE GOT NEWS FOR YOU vWH/FOUR BROTHERS/BIJOU   (17)

same location, November 6, 1948

ROMANCE IN THE DARK vMAM/JOHN HAD THE NUMBER/FLAMINGO/BOOMSIE   (17)

WOODY HERMAN AND HIS ORCHESTRA — EARLY AUTUMN
Personnel as for October 30, except that Red Rodney (tp) replaces Irvin Markowitz.

Los Angeles, December 29, 1948

LEMON DROP -1/THAT'S RIGHT
- 1: Scat bop vocal by Shorty Rogers, Terry Gibbs and Chubby Jackson

Los Angeles, December 30, 1948

EARLY AUTUMN/KEEPER OF THE FLAME

Al Porcino, Stan Fishelson, Charlie Walp, Shorty Rogers, Ernie Royal (tp), Ollie Wilson, Earl Swope, Bill Harris, Bart Varsalona (tb), Woody Herman (cl, as), Sam Marowitz (as), Jimmy Giuffre, Gene Ammons, Buddy Savitt (ts), Serge Chaloff (bs), Terry Gibbs (vb), Lou Levy (p), Oscar Pettiford (b), Shelly Manne (d).

New York, May 26, 1949

MORE MOON

Los Angeles, July 14, 1949

NOT REALLY THE BLUES
Joe Mondragon (b) replaces Oscar Pettiford.

Los Angeles, July 20, 1949

LOLLYPOP -1/TENDERLY
- 1: Scat bop vocal by Shorty Rogers, Terry Gibbs and Woody Herman

Los Angeles, July 21, 1949

RHAPSODY IN WOOD/THE GREAT LIE

Don Ferrara, Rolf Ericson, Doug Mettome, Conte Candoli (tp), Herb Randel, Jerry Dorn, Bill Harris (tb), Woody Herman (cl, as), Phil Urso, Buddy Wise, Bob Graf (ts), Marty Flax (bs), Dave McKenna (p), Red Mitchell (b), Sonny Igoe (d).

Nashville, June 25, 1950

MUSIC TO DANCE TO/SONNY SPEAKS

Vern Friley (tb) replaces Bill Harris.   *Chicago, August 9, 1950*
STARLIGHT SOUVENIRS

CAPITOL (H) 5C 052 80805/CAPITOL (A) M-11034

WOODY HERMAN AND HIS ORCHESTRA — MEN FROM MARS
(American issue)/HEY! HEARD THE HERD? (French issue)
John Howell, Jack Scarda, Roy Caton, Don Fagerquist (tp), Jack Green, Carl Fontana, Urbie Green (tb), Woody Herman (cl, as), Dick Hafer, Arno Marsh, Bill Perkins (ts), Sam Staff (bs), Nat Pierce (p, cls), Chubby Jackson (b), Sonny Igoe (d).   *New York, May 30, 1952*

TERESSITA/STOMPIN' AT THE SAVOY

Lee Fortier (tp) replaces Jack Scarda.   *New York, July 7, 1952*
CELESTIAL BLUES/PERDIDO/MOTEN STOMP

Phil Cook, Roy Caton, Tommy DiCarlo, Dick Sherman, Stu Williamson (tp), Jack Green, Will Bradley, Carl Fontana (tb), Woody Herman (cl), Dick Hafer, Arno Marsh, Bill Perkins (ts), Sam Staff (bs), Nat Pierce (p, cls), Chubby Jackson (b), Art Mardigan (d). *New York, January 13, 1953*
BLUE LOU/WOOFTIE

Joe Burnett, Roy Caton, Tommy DiCarlo, Stu Williamson (tp), Jack Green, Carl Fontana, Urbie Green (tb), Dick Hafer, Arno Marsh, Bill Trujillo (ts), Sam Staff (bs), Nat Pierce (p, organo), Red Kelly (b), Art Mardigan (d), Woody Herman (leader). *New York, May 14, 1953*
MEN FROM MARS

Bernie Glow, Ernie Royal, Harold Wegbreit, Bobby Styles, Stu Williamson (tp), Vern Friley, Urbie Green, Frank Rehak, Kai Winding (tb), Jerry Coker, Dick Hafer, Bill Trujillo (ts), Sam Staff (bs), Nat Pierce (p), Red Kelly (b), Art Mardigan (d), Woody Herman (leader). *New York, September 11, 1953*
FOUR OTHERS

John Howell, Bernie Glow, Jim Bonebrake, Reuben McFall (tp), Dick Kenney, Jim Hewitt, Frank Rehak, Kai Winding (tb), Woody Herman (cl), Jerry Coker, Dick Hafer, Bill Trujillo (ts), Sam Staff (f), Nat Pierce (p), Red Kelly (b), Art Mardigan (d). *New York, October 5, 1953*
MARAKEESH

Al Porcino, John Howell, Bill Castagnino, Reuben McFall, Dick Collins (tp), Cy Touff (btp), Dick Kenney, Keith Moon (tb), Woody Herman (cl, as), Jerry Coker, Dick Hafer, Bill Perkins (ts), Jack Nimitz (bs), Nat Pierce (p), Red Kelly (b), Chuck Flores (d). *New York, March 20, 1954*
CASTLE ROCK -1/MAMBO THE MOST (Parts 1 & 2)
- 1: Sam Taylor (ts) and Mickey Baker (g) added; Lloyd Trotman (b) and Panama Francis (d) replace Red Kelly and Chuck Flores
VERVE (A) MGV-8216/VERVE (F) 2304 509

WOODY HERMAN AND HIS ORCHESTRA — THE WOODY HERMAN BAND!
Al Porcino, John Howell, Bill Castagnino, Charlie Walp, Dick Collins (tp), Cy Touff (btp), Dick Kenney, Keith Moon (tb), Woody Herman (cl, as), Dave Madden, Dick Hafer, Bill Perkins (ts), Jack Nimitz (bs), Nat Pierce (p), Red Kelly (b), Chuck Flores (d). *Los Angeles, September 8, 1954*
MISTY MORNING/BOO HOO/HITTIN' THE BOTTLE

Los Angeles, September 9, 1954

BY PLAY

Los Angeles, September 13, 1954

LA CUCARACHA MAMBO

Los Angeles, September 24, 1954

AUTOBAHN BLUES/SLEEP/ILL WIND/WOULD HE

104

STRANGE/WILD APPLE HONEY

Los Angeles, September 25, 1954

CAPITOL (A) T560/CAPITOL (E) LCT 6014

WOODY HERMAN AND HIS ORCHESTRA — ROAD BAND!

Personnel as for September 8, except that Richie Kamuca (ts) replaces Dave Madden. *Chicago, October 13, 1954*

I'LL NEVER BE THE SAME/GINA

Jerry Kail, Gerry LaFurn, Bernie Glow, Reuben McFall, Charlie Walp, Dick Collins (tp), Cy Touff (btp), Dick Kenney, Keith Moon (tb), Woody Herman (cl, as), Dick Hafer, Richie Kamuca, Art Pirie (ts), Jack Nimitz (bs), Nat Pierce (p), Billy Bauer (g), John Beal (b), Chuck Flores (d).

New York, June 6, 1955

OPUS DE FUNK/COOL CAT ON A HOT TIN ROOF/PIMLICO

Nick Travis (tp) replaces Bernie Glow. *same date*

CAPTAIN AHAB/I REMEMBER DUKE

Nick Travis (tp) omitted. *New York, June 7, 1955*

SENTIMENTAL JOURNEY/WHERE OR WHEN   CAPITOL (A) T658

Note: This album was issued in the U.K. on three extended play records —Capitol (E) EAP1009, EAP2-658 and EAP3-658

WOODY HERMAN AND THE LAS VEGAS HERD — JACKPOT!

Johnny Coppola, Dick Collins (tp), Cy Touff (btp), Woody Herman (cl), Richie Kamuca (ts), Norman Pockrandt (p), Monty Budwig (b), Chuck Flores (d).

Los Angeles, December 1, 1955

9.20 SPECIAL/JUMPIN' AT THE WOODSIDE/BAGS' OTHER GROOVE/BASS FACE/THE BOOT/WAILING WALL/JUNIOR/BROADWAY

CAPITOL (A & E) T748

WOODY HERMAN AND HIS ORCHESTRA — BLUES GROOVE

Personnel as for December 1; Woody Herman also (v).

Los Angeles, December 5, 1955

EVERYDAY I'VE GOT THE BLUES vWH/BASIN STREET BLUES vWH

Johnny Coppola, Burt Collins, Bill Castagnino, Dud Harvey, Dick Collins (tp), Wayne Andre, Bill Harris, Bobby Lamb (tb), Woody Herman (cl, as, v), Bob Hardaway, Richie Kamuca, Arno Marsh (ts), Jay Cameron (bs), Vic Feldman (vb, cga), Vince Guaraldi (p), Remo Biondi (g), Monty Budwig (b), Gus Gustafson (d). *Chicago, May 15, 1956*

CALL IT STORMY MONDAY vWH/SMACK DAB IN THE MIDDLE vWH/PINETOP'S BLUES vWH/TROUBLE IN MIND vWH/BLUES GROOVE/DUPREE BLUES vWH

Chicago, May 16, 1956

I WANT A LITTLE GIRL vWH   CAPITOL (A & E) T784

WOODY HERMAN AND HIS ORCHESTRA — WOODY HERMAN '58
(American issue)/**JAZZ, THE UTMOST!** (British issue)
Johnny Coppola, Andy Peele, Bill Castagnino, Danny Styles, Bill Berry (tp), Willie
Dennis, Bill Harris, Bobby Lamb (tb), Woody Herman (cl, as), Jimmy Cook, Jay
Migliori, Bob Newman (ts), Roger Pemberton (bs), John Bunch (p), Jim Gannon
(b), Don Michaels (d).   *New York, July 2, 1957*
BLUE SATIN/READY, GET SET, JUMP/BAR FLY BLUES/ROLAND'S ROLLIN'/THE
PREACHER/WAILIN' IN THE WOODSHED/DOWNWIND/WHY YOU

New York, July 3, 1957
STAIRWAY TO THE BLUES/GENE'S STRUT/SMALL CREVICE/TRY TO FORGET
VERVE (A) MGV-8255/COLUMBIA (E) 33CX10129

WOODY HERMAN AND HIS ORCHESTRA — THE HERD RIDES AGAIN
Al Stewart, Bernie Glow, Nick Travis, Irvin Markowitz, Ernie Royal (tp), Billy
Byers, Frank Rehak, Bob Brookmeyer (tb), Woody Herman (cl, as, v), Sam
Marowitz (as), Al Cohn, Sam Donahue, Paul Quinichette (ts), Danny Bank (bs),
Nat Pierce (p), Billy Bauer (g), Chubby Jackson (b), Don Lamond (d).
New York, July 30, 1958
NORTHWEST PASSAGE/CALDONIA vWH/WILD ROOT/THE GOOD EARTH/BLOWIN' UP A
STORM/I COVER THE WATERFRONT

Burt Collins and Bernie Privin (tp) replace Bernie Glow and Nick Travis.
New York, August 1, 1958
IT'S COOLIN' TIME/CRAZY RHYTHM/SINBAD THE TAILOR/FIRE ISLAND/BLACK
ORCHID/BIJOU
EVEREST (A) BR-5003 (SDBR-1003)/TOP RANK (E) 35/038

WOODY HERMAN AND HIS ANGLO-AMERICAN HERD
Reunald Jones, Bert Courtley, Les Condon, Kenny Wheeler, Nat Adderley (tp), Bill
Harris, Eddie Harvey, Ken Wray (tb), Woody Herman (cl, as), Johnny Scott, Art
Ellefson, Don Rendell (ts), Ronnie Ross (bs), Vince Guaraldi (p), Charlie Byrd (g),
Keeter Betts (b), Jimmy Campbell (d).
Free Trade Hall, Manchester, April 18, 1959
THE PREACHER/LIKE SOME BLUES, MAN, LIKE/FROM PILLAR TO POST/FOUR
BROTHERS/OPUS DE FUNK/EARLY AUTUMN/PLAYGIRL STROLL/AT THE
WOODCHOPPER'S BALL
JAZZ GROOVE (E) 004

WOODY HERMAN'S BIG NEW HERD AT THE MONTEREY JAZZ FESTIVAL
Al Porcino, Bill Chase, Frank Huggins, Ray Linn, Conte Candoli (tp), Sy Zentner,
Urbie Green, Bill Smiley (tb), Woody Herman (cl), Don Lanphere (as, ts), Richie
Kamuca, Bill Perkins, Zoot Sims (ts), Med Flory (bs), Vic Feldman (p, vb), Charlie
Byrd (g), Monty Budwig (b), Mel Lewis (d).
Monterey, California, October 3, 1959
FOUR BROTHERS/LIKE SOME BLUES, MAN, LIKE/SKOOBEEDOOBEE/MONTEREY APPLE

TREE/SKYLARK/THE MAGPIE

ATLANTIC (A) LP1328 (SD1328)/
LONDON (E) LTZ-K 15200 (SAH-K 6100)

Note: This album has also been issued with the title *The Magpie.*

WOODY HERMAN AND HIS ORCHESTRA — THE NEW SWINGIN' HERMAN HERD

Bill Chase, Paul Fontaine, Don Rader, Jimmy Bennett, Rolf Ericson (tp), Jimmy Guinn, George Hanna, Kent McGarity (tb), Woody Herman (cl, as), Don Lanphere, Larry McKenna (ts), Gus Maas (ts, f), Jimmy Mosher (bs), Martin Harris (p), Larry Rockwell (b), Jimmy Campbell (d).

Chicago, March 22, 1960

MONTMARTRE BUS RIDE/ARUBA/DARN THAT DREAM/CROWN ROYAL/I CAN'T GET STARTED/THE GRIND/OFF SHORE/SINGLE O/AFTERGLOW/HERMOSA BEACH

CROWN (A) CLP5180 (CST205)/
EROS (E) ERL 50027 (ERLS 50027)

WOODY HERMAN : 1963

Bill Chase, Paul Fontaine, Ziggy Harrell, Dave Gale, Gerry Lamy (tp), Phil Wilson, Eddie Morgan, Jack Gale (tb), Woody Herman (cl, as, v), Gordon Brisker, Larry Cavelli, Sal Nistico (ts), Gene Allen (bs), Nat Pierce (p), Chuck Andrus (b), Jake Hanna (d). *New York, October 15, 1962*

MO-LASSES/SISTER SADIE/SIG EP

New York, October 16, 1962

CAMEL WALK vWH/IT'S A LONESOME OLD TOWN/BLUES FOR J.P./DON'T GET AROUND MUCH ANYMORE/TUNIN' IN

PHILIPS (A) PHM200-065 (PHS600-065)/
PHILIPS (E) 652 025 BL (852 025 BY)

ENCORE : WOODY HERMAN — 1963

Bill Chase, Billy Hunt, Paul Fontaine, Dave Gale, Gerry Lamy (tp), Phil Wilson, Henry Southall, Bob Rudolph (tb), Woody Herman (cl, as, v), Bobby Jones, Bill Perkins, Sal Nistico (ts), Frank Hittner (bs), Nat Pierce (p), Chuck Andrus (b), Jake Hanna (d). *Basin Street West, Los Angeles, May 19, 20 & 21, 1963*

WATERMELON MAN/DAYS OF WINE AND ROSES/EL TORO GRANDE/JAZZ ME BLUES/ BODY AND SOUL/THAT'S WHERE IT IS/BETTER GET IT IN YOUR SOUL/CALDONIA vWH

PHILIPS (A) PHM200-092 (PHS600-092)/
PHILIPS (E) BL7574 (SBL7574)

Note: Further material recorded at this engagement was issued on another album — see below

WOODY HERMAN : 1964

Bill Chase, Billy Hunt, Paul Fontaine, Gerry Lamy, Danny Nolan (tp), Phil Wilson, Henry Southall, Kenny Wenzel (tb), Woody Herman (cl, as), Carmen Leggio, Sal Nistico, John Stevens (ts), Nick Brignola (bs), Nat Pierce (p), Chuck Andrus (b), Jake Hanna (d). *New York, November 20, 1963*

HALLELUJAH TIME/DEEP PURPLE/MY WISH

New York, November 22, 1963

JAZZ HOOT/A TASTE OF HONEY/THE STRUT/SATIN DOLL

AFTER YOU'VE GONE/COUSINS · PHILIPS (A) PHM200-118 (PHS600-118)/
PHILIPS (E) BL7608 (SBL7608)

WOODY HERMAN — WOODY'S BIG BAND GOODIES
Personnel as previously listed for the following engagement:
Basin Street West, Los Angeles, May 19, 20 & 21, 1963
WAILIN' IN THE WOODSHED/THE GOOD EARTH/SIDEWALKS OF CUBA/I CAN'T GET
STARTED/BIJOU/APPLE HONEY

Bill Chase, Billy Hunt, Dusko Goykovich, Gerry Lamy, Lawrence Ford (tp), Phil
Wilson, Henry Southall, Bob Stroup (tb), Woody Herman (cl, as), Andy McGhee,
Raoul Romero, Gary Klein (ts), Tom Anastas (bs), Nat Pierce (p), Chuck Andrus
(b), Jake Hanna (d).
Harrah's Club, Lake Tahoe, Nevada, September 9, 1964
BLUE MONK/YOU DIRTY DOG/POUR HOUSE BLUES
PHILIPS (A) PHM200-171 (PHS600-171)/
LIMELIGHT (E) LML4007 (SLML4007)

WOODY HERMAN — THE SWINGING HERMAN HERD RECORDED LIVE
Personnel as listed above for the following engagement:
Harrah's Club, Lake Tahoe, Nevada, September 9, 1964
THE GOOD LIFE/BEDROOM EYES/THE THINGS WE SAID TODAY/JUST SQUEEZE ME/
WHAT KIND OF FOOL AM I? -1/DR WONG'S BAG/EVERYBODY LOVES SOMEBODY/WA-WA
BLUES -1/DEAR JOHN C
- 1: Joe Carroll (v) added
PHILIPS (A) PHM200-131 (PHS600-131)/
PHILIPS (E) BL7649) (SBL7649)

WOODY HERMAN — WOODY'S WINNERS
Bill Chase, Don Rader, Bobby Shew, Dusko Goykovich, Gerry Lamy (tp), Henry
Southall, Frank Tesinsky, Donald Doane (tb), Woody Herman (cl, as, ss), Gary
Klein, Andy McGhee, Sal Nistico (ts), Tom Anastas (bs), Nat Pierce (p), Tony
Leonardi (b), Ronnie Zito (d).
Basin Street West, San Francisco, June 28, 29 & 30, 1965
23 RED/MY FUNNY VALENTINE/NORTHWEST PASSAGE/POOR BUTTERFLY/GREASY SACK
BLUES/WOODY'S WHISTLE/RED ROSES FOR A BLUE LADY/OPUS DE FUNK + BLUE FLAME
COLUMBIA (A) CL2436 (CS9236)/CBS (E) BPG62619 (SBPG62619)

WOODY HERMAN — JAZZ HOOT
Same personnel and dates as last.
I CAN'T GET STARTED/HALLELUJAH TIME/SATIN DOLL/JAZZ HOOT/WATERMELON
MAN/GREASY SACK BLUES*
* This version of *Greasy Sack Blues* is the same as that on the *Woody's Winners* album.

Bill Chase, Bill Byrne, Ziggy Harrell, Alex Rodriguez, Paul Fontaine (tp), Henry
Southall, Jerry Collins, Gary Potter (tb), Woody Herman (cl, as), Andy McGhee,

Frank Foster, Louis Orenstein (ts), Tom Anastas (bs), Nat Pierce (p), Tony Leonardi (b), Ronnie Zito (d). *New York, October 8, 1965*
SUMPTUOUS/THE BLACK OPAL

Bill Chase, Marvin Stamm, Bill Byrne, Dave Gale, Lyn Biviano (tp), Henry Southall, Carl Fontana, Jerry Collins (tb), Frank Vicari, Bob Pierson, Sal Nistico (ts), Tom Anastas (bs), Nat Pierce (p), Mike Moore (b), Ronnie Zito (d), Woody Herman (v). *New York, July 7, 1966*
SIDEWINDER vWH

Bill Byrne, Lloyd Michaels, Lyn Biviano, Dick Rudebusch, John Crews (tp), Jim Foy, Mel Wanzo, Bill Watrous (tb), Woody Herman (cl, as, v), Al Gibbons, Steve Marcus, Bob Pierson (ts), Joe Temperley (bs), Mike Alterman (p), Bob Daugherty (b), Ronnie Zito (d). *New York, March 23, 1967*
THE DUCK - l/BOOPSIE vWH
- 1: Charlie Byrd (g) added as featured soloist
COLUMBIA (A) PC32530/CBS (E) S80248

WOODY LIVE — EAST AND WEST
Personnel as previously listed for the following engagement:
Basin Street West, San Francisco, June 28, 29 & 30, 1965
I REMEMBER CLIFFORD/WALTZ FOR A HUNG-UP BALLET MISTRESS/THE PREACHER

Personnel as for March 23, 1967.
Riverboat Room, New York, March 25, 1967
FREE AGAIN/MAKE SOMEONE HAPPY/TOMORROW'S BLUES TODAY/FOUR BROTHERS (REVISITED)/COUSINS COLUMBIA (A) CL2693 (CS9496)/
CBS (E) BPG63099 (SBPG63099)

WOODY HERMAN — LIGHT MY FIRE
Gary Grant, Nat Pavone, Henry Hall, Sal Marguez, James Bossert (tp), Bobby Burgess, Henry Southall, Vince Prudente (tb), Woody Herman (cl, as, ss), Frank Vicari, Sal Nistico, Steve Lederer (ts), Tom Boras (bs), John Hicks (p), Phil Upchurch (g), Arthur Harper (eb), Ed Soph (d), Morris Jennings (pc).
Chicago, October 1968
PONTIEO/HERE I AM, BABY/HARD TO KEEP MY MIND ON YOU/MACARTHUR PARK (Parts 1 & 2)/LIGHT MY FIRE/I SAY A LITTLE PRAYER/HUSH/FOR LOVE OF IVY/ IMPRESSION OF STRAYHORN/KEEP ON KEEPIN' ON
CADET (A) LP819 (LPS819)/CHESS (E) 6310 127

WOODY HERMAN — THE RAVEN SPEAKS
Al Porcino, Bill Byrne (tp), Charles Davis, John Thomas, Bill Stapleton (tp, flh), Bobby Burgess, Rick Stepton, Harold Garrett (tb), Woody Herman (ss, cl, as), Frank Tiberi, Greg Herbert (ts, ww), Steve Lederer (ts), Tom Anastas (bs), Harold Danko (ep), Pat Martino (g), Al Johnson (eb), Joe LaBarbera (d), John Pacheco (cga). *New York, August 28, 29 & 30, 1972*
FAT MAMA/ALONE AGAIN (NATURALLY)/SANDIA CHICANO (WATERMELON MAN)/IT'S TOO LATE/THE RAVEN SPEAKS/SUMMER OF '42/REUNION AT NEWPORT 1972/BILL'S BLUES FANTASY (A) 9416/
FANTASY (E) FT509

WOODY HERMAN — GIANT STEPS

Bill Byrne, Larry Pyatt, Gil Rathel, Walt Blanton (tp), Bill Stapleton (tp, flh), Jim Pugh, Geoff Sharp, Harold Garrett (tb), Woody Herman (ss, as, cl), Frank Tiberi, Steve Lederer (ts), Greg Herbert (ts, ww), Harry Kleintank (ts, bs), Andy Laverne (ep), Joe Beck (g), Wayne Darling (b, eb), Ed Soph (d), Ray Barretto (cga).

New York, April 9, 11 & 12, 1973

LA FIESTA/A SONG FOR YOU/FREEDOM JAZZ DANCE/THE MEANING OF THE BLUES/THE FIRST THING I DO/THINK ON ME/GIANT STEPS/A CHILD IS BORN/BEBOP AND ROSES

FANTASY (A) 9432

WOODY HERMAN — THUNDERING HERD

Bill Byrne (tp), Dave Strahl, Buddy Powers, Bill Stapleton, Tony Klatka (tp, flh), Jim Pugh, Steve Kohlbacher, Harold Garrett (tb), Woody Herman (as, ss), Frank Tiberi, Greg Herbert, Gary Anderson (ts, ww), Jan Konopasek (bs), Andy Laverne (p), Chip Jackson (eb), Ron Davis (d), John Rae (pc).

Berkeley, California, January 2, 3 & 4, 1974

LAZY BIRD/BLUES FOR POLAND/WHAT ARE YOU DOING THE REST OF YOUR LIFE?/ NAIMA/CORAZON - 1/COME SATURDAY MORNING/BASS FOLK SONG - 1

- 1: Richard Dollarhide (cga) added

FANTASY (A) 9452/
FANTASY (E) FT 521

WOODY HERMAN — 40TH ANNIVERSARY CARNEGIE HALL CONCERT

Alan Vizutti, Bill Byrne, Nelson Hatt, John Hoffman, Dennis Dotson (tp), Jim Pugh, Dale Kirkland, Jim Daniels (tb), Woody Herman (cl, as, ss, v), Frank Tiberi, Gary Anderson, Joe Lovano (ts, f, cl), John Oslawski (bs), Pat Coil (p), Rusty Holloway (b), Dan D'Imperio (d).

Carnegie Hall, New York, November 20, 1976

PENNY ARCADE/CRISIS/SHE'S GONE/FANFARE FOR THE COMMON MAN/BLUES IN THE NIGHT vWH

Each of the titles from this concert listed below features at least one of the following Woody Herman alumni as guests (details are given in the sleeve notes):-
Pete Candoli, Conte Candoli, Danny Stiles (tp), Phil Wilson (tb), Sam Marowitz (as), Al Cohn, Stan Getz, Jimmy Giuffre, Flip Phillips, Zoot Sims (ts), Ralph Burns, Jimmy Rowles, Nat Pierce (p), Billy Bauer (g), Chubby Jackson (b), Don Lamond, Jake Hanna (d), Mary Ann McCall (v).

APPLE HONEY/SWEET AND LOVELY/FOUR BROTHERS/BROTHERHOOD OF MAN/EARLY AUTUMN/WRAP YOUR TROUBLES IN DREAMS vMAM/EVERYWHERE/BIJOU/COUSINS/ BLUE SERGE/BLUE GETZ BLUES/CALDONIA vWH

RCA PL02203 (double album)

WOODY HERMAN — WOODY AND FRIENDS

Joe Rodriguez, Tim Burke, Kitt Reid (tp), Bill Byrne, Jim Powell (tp, flh), Birch Johnson, Nelson Hinds, Larry Shunk (tb), Woody Herman (ss, as), Frank Tiberi, Dick Mitchell (ts, ww), Bob Belden (ts), Gary Smulyan (bs), Dave Lalama (p), Dave Larocca (b), Ed Soph (d).

Monterey, California, September 15, 1979
CARAVAN/I GOT IT BAD/COUNT DOWN/BETTER GET IT IN YOUR SOUL/WHAT ARE YOU DOING THE REST OF YOUR LIFE? -1/WOODY 'N' YOU -2/MANTECA -2
- 1: Stan Getz (ts) added as featured soloist
- 2: Dizzy Gillespie, Woody Shaw (tp) and Slide Hampton (tb) added as featured soloists   CONCORD (A) CJ-170

WOODY HERMAN PRESENTS FOUR OTHERS
Woody Herman (as -1, leader), Al Cohn, Sal Nistico, Bill Perkins, Flip Phillips (ts), John Bunch (p), George Duvivier (b), Don Lamond (d).
New York, July 22, 1981
NOT REALLY THE BLUES/WOODY'S LAMENT/TINY'S BLUES/I WANNA GO HOME/LOOSE ABBERATIONS/FOUR OTHERS/TENDERLY -1/THE GOOF AND I
CONCORD (A) CJ-180

THE WOODY HERMAN BIG BAND — LIVE AT THE CONCORD JAZZ FESTIVAL
Bill Stapleton, Brian O'Flaherty, George Rabbai, Scott Wagstaff, Mark Lewis (tp), Gene Smith, Larry Shunk, John Fedchock (tb), Woody Herman (cl, as), Paul McGinley, Bill Ross, Randy Russell (ts, ww), Mike Brignola (bs), John Oddo (p, ep), Mike Hall (b, eb), Dave Ratajczak (d, pc).
Monterey, California, August 15, 1981
THINGS AIN'T WHAT THEY USED TO BE -1/THEME IN SEARCH OF A MOVIE/MIDNIGHT RUN/YOU ARE SO BEAUTIFUL/JOHN BROWN'S OTHER BODY/ESPECIALLY FOR YOU/ NORTH BEACH BREAKDOWN/THE DOLPHIN -2/LEMON DROP -1, 3
- 1: Al Cohn (ts) added
- 2: Stan Getz (ts) added as featured soloist
- 3: Scat bop vocal by George Rabbai   CONCORD (A) CJ-191

WOODY HERMAN — WORLD CLASS
Bill Byrne, Brian O'Flaherty, George Rabbai, Scott Wagstaff, Mark Lewis (tp), Gene Smith, Randy Hawes, John Fedchock (tb), Woody Herman (cl, as, ss), Frank Tiberi, Jim Carroll (ts), Paul MicGinley (ts, f), Mike Brignola (bs), John Oddo (p), Dave Shapiro (b), Dave Ratajczak (d).
Osaka Festival Hall, September 1982
FOUR BROTHERS -1/THE CLAW -1/PEANUT VENDOR -2/CRYSTAL SILENCE -2/GREASY SACK BLUES/PERDIDO -3
- 1: Al Cohn, Med Flory, Sal Nistico and Flip Phillips (ts) added
- 2: Jeff Hamilton (pc) added
- 3: Flip Phillips (ts) added

Woody Herman, George Rabbai (v).   *Yokohama Stadium, September 1982*
ROCKIN' CHAIR vWH & GR

Al Cohn, Sal Nistico (ts) added.   *The Budokan, Tokyo, September 1982*
WOODY'S LAMENT   CONCORD (A) CJ-240

Key to Records Listed

for items recorded before December 1948

(1)	**THE BAND THAT PLAYS THE BLUES**	
		Ace Of Hearts (E) AH156
(2)	**WOODY HERMAN 1937**	Hindsight (A) HSR116,
		London (E) HMA5048
(3)	**GOLDEN FAVOURITES**	Decca (A) DL8133,
		Ace Of Hearts (E) AH78
(4)	**THE BAND THAT PLAYS THE BLUES**	Affinity (E) AFS1008
(5)	**DANCE TIME — FORTY-THREE**	First Heard (E) FH34
(6)	**THE TURNING POINT**	Coral (E) CP2
(7)	**WOODY HERMAN AND HIS FIRST HERD 1944**	
		Hindsight (A) HSR134,
		London (E) HMA5058
(8)	**WOODY HERMAN AND THE WOODCHOPPERS 'FAN IT'**	
		Swing House (E) SWH19
(9)	**THE FIRST HERD**	Fanfare (A) 22-122
(10)	**THE FIRST HERD LIVE IN HI FI**	Fanfare (A) 43-143
(11)	**THE THUNDERING HERDS VOLUME 1**	CBS (E) BPG62158
(12)	**THE THUNDERING HERDS VOLUME 2**	CBS (E) BPG62159
(13)	**THE THUNDERING HERDS VOLUME 3**	CBS (E) BPG62160

The above three discs were issued as a boxed set on Columbia (A) C3L25

(14)	**WOODY HERMAN AT CARNEGIE HALL**	Verve (E) 2317 031
(15)	**WOODY HERMAN AT THE HOLLYWOOD PALLADIUM 1948**	Hep (E) 7
(16)	**WOODY HERMAN ROADBAND 1948**	Hep (E) 18
(17)	**BILL HARRIS & SERGE CHALOFF & WOODY HERMAN**	Alto (A) AL705